MARK TWAIN'S
FABLE OF PROGRESS:
Political and Economic Ideas in
"A Connecticut Yankee"

by HENRY NASH SMITH

Rutgers University Press
New Brunswick, New Jersey

CONTENTS

The 1963 Brown and Haley Lectures are the eleventh of a series that has been given annually at the University of Puget Sound, Tacoma, Washington, by a scholar distinguished for his work in the Social Studies or the Humanities. The purpose of these lectures is to present original analyses of some intellectual problems confronting the present age.

MARK TWAIN'S FABLE OF PROGRESS

PREFACE

In *Mark Twain: The Development of a Writer*, published in 1962, I devoted a chapter to the problems of literary technique involved in the composition of *A Connecticut Yankee in King Arthur's Court*. The chapter cost me more effort than any other, and it now seems the least satisfactory part of my book. *A Connecticut Yankee* has remained in my mind as a piece of unfinished business, seeming more and more problematical. I had asserted that the writing of this fable coincided with and perhaps precipitated in Mark Twain something like a negative conversion, a loss of faith in progress and human perfectibility which all but paralyzed his powers of imagination and condemned him to the relative sterility of his last twenty years. An event of this magnitude is obviously not produced by clear and simple causes, and I do not imagine that I fully understand it even yet. But I welcomed the invitation to deliver the Brown & Haley Lectures at the

University of Puget Sound because it gave me an opportunity to examine once again what I regard as the crucial problem in Mark Twain's career as a writer.

My earlier analysis had considered Hank Morgan, the protagonist of the story, in the long series of vernacular characters culminating in Huck Finn. This approach still seems valid to me, but I have become aware of another aspect of Mark Twain's thought which has led me to place Hank Morgan in a different context, to see him as a member also of the numerous company of businessmen in nineteenth-century American fiction. He is a vernacular hero but also a capitalist hero. He needs to be considered not only in relation to Huck Finn but to other fictional portraits of the entrepreneur and executive as a type.

This line of inquiry could obviously lead at least as far back as Poor Richard and the "I" of Franklin's *Autobiography*. But in the three lectures that have become chapters in this book I could not undertake so long an excursion. I have accordingly narrowed my discussion of other businessmen in fiction to two novels by friends of Mark Twain published in the same year with *A Connecticut Yankee*, hoping in this fashion to suggest the framework of assumptions within which, or in defiance of which, he conceived his version of the capitalist hero. In the second chapter I trace the growth of *A Connecticut Yankee* in the writer's mind. This is a fascinating exercise because we have unusually full information about the stages through which the book

4

passed before it reached its final form. In the third chapter I consider the major ideas in the story, especially the theory of progress and the interpretation of capitalism Mark Twain sets forth in it.

My analysis has led me to dwell upon the inconsistencies in thought and technique that mar a potential masterpiece. My vision of what it might have become has perhaps made me unduly severe in dealing with the story that Mark Twain actually wrote. If I seem to regard it as on the whole a failure, I hope I have demonstrated that it is the failure of a great writer, and therefore both interesting and important.

I must apologize for the necessity of taking up here again some of the evidence I have discussed earlier. I trust that the present study places this evidence in a new context.

I wish to thank President R. Franklin Thompson of the University of Puget Sound and Professor Lyle S. Shelmidine, Chairman of the Committee on the Brown & Haley Lectures, for their invitation to occupy a chair that has had such distinguished occupants in previous years; and to express my pleasure in conversations with students and members of the faculty of the University during my visit to the campus in April 1963.

H. N. S.

Berkeley
June 1963

I. BACKGROUND: *The Businessman and the Genteel Tradition*

I

Mark Twain's *A Connecticut Yankee in King Arthur's Court* (1889) is one of the most characteristic productions of the decade when Americans generally first realized they were entering the modern world. The Civil War had given a decided impetus to the mechanization of industry in this country, and the process had gained speed in the post-Civil War decades. By the 1880's a revolutionary change began to be apparent to most people in the United States—not only factory workers and dwellers in the industrial cities, but also farmers, especially in the West, who were using machines to expand agricultural production and found themselves dependent on the new railway systems to send their crops to markets in the East and in Europe. The pace and scope of industrialization placed unprecedented strains on American society and American culture. The traditional system of values, the beliefs about men, institutions, and the universe that had guided the lives of earlier generations, were coming to seem irrelevant. New conceptions of value, a new ethics, a new philosophy had to be created. As always, imaginative writers had the task of synthesizing fact and theory into images that could be understood by the public at large. Mark Twain's *A Connecticut Yankee* is an effort to perform this task. Although it is basically comic in conception and contains some of his most irresistible humor, it is of all Mark Twain's books the most urgently focused on the state of the nation and of the world at the moment of writing. The burlesque tale expresses a philosophy of history and a theory of the capitalist system created by the industrial revolution—and the story breaks under the pressure of the thought and emotion that the writer poured into it.

Mark Twain wrote *A Connecticut Yankee* between 1886 and 1889, at the peak of a public debate over the issues of industrialism. Lyle A. Rose, the leading bibliographer of the period, has noted that in the early 1880's novels dealing with economic and political problems were for the first time more numerous than any other sort of "purpose-novel." Furthermore, "a dozen major nonfiction treatises published in those years still live; and many men at that time grew conscious of the interconnections among such phenomena as strikes, technological unemployment, land problems, the tariff, the 'octopus-like' nature of monopoly, the domination of politics by business, and some of the main difficulties encountered by civil service reform and other panaceas." [1]

This list of problems has a familiar ring. Of course to bring it up to date we should have to add a long list of twentieth-century difficulties in international affairs. The blessed indifference of Mark Twain's contemporaries to what was going on outside the boundaries of the United States seems to place them in another world from ours. But except for civil-service reform, which was a heritage from the patronage battles of the pre-Civil War era, the items under public debate in the 1880's are duplicated in any copy of a newspaper in the 1960's. These are the problems created by industrialization. In the 1880's they were relatively new, but they are still actively present; the external questions that face the American Empire of the mid-twentieth century have merely been added to the main domestic issues of the post-Civil War decades.

What was happening then has been summed up in the title of a standard historical work as the triumph of American capitalism. The history of the term is itself suggestive. Just as the word "individualism" had been introduced into the American vocabulary in the age of Jackson, so a writer for the *North American Review* in 1886 made the first recorded use of the word "capitalism" in the sense of "the concentration of wealth in the hands of a few; the power or influence of large or concentrated capital." [2] The context is worth quoting: "The working-men find the journals out of sympathy

with their aims and aspirations, and have learnt to regard them as hopelessly subservient to what they call
'capitalism.'" When the word first became current in
this country, it was a polemic term used by workers
who felt themselves menaced by the emergent industrial system, particularly by the power of the new captains of industry. The triumph of industrialism brought
with it conflict—a national economic cleavage which
tended to replace the sectional tensions preceding the
Civil War.

It would be easy to multiply examples of attacks on
the new economic order by the many dissidents and
radical spokesmen who became vocal during the decade. In 1879 Henry George had declared that industrialization and urbanization—the effects of what was
almost universally called "progress"—were threats to
individual liberty. A decade later the novelist Albion
W. Tourgée, a convert to Christian Socialism, summed
up what had become the commonplaces of left-wing
criticism:

> To-day's conditions—its material tendency and devel-
> opment—have opposed the fulfillment of yesterday's as-
> piration. The most tremendous forces have moved with
> unprecedented energy toward the subjection of the in-
> dividual. During the last half-century, the segregation
> of capital in a few hands has been equaled only by the
> restriction of opportunity. . . . Organization has prac-
> tically eradicated the individual. The small manufac-
> turer has almost disappeared. The small dealer has been

9

absorbed. The small manufacturer has become a foreman; the small merchant an agent. . . . Already a new
feudalism has been developed in which power is trans-
mitted, not by blood, but by bequest, and in which vas-
salage is secured, not by an oath of allegiance, but by
dependency. . . . Those who serve and those who control are being separated by sharper lines and more inflexible barriers.[3]

The fact that the growth of mechanized industry
had tended to centralize economic power was recognized by defenders as well as attackers. In 1889 Andrew Carnegie, asserting that the essence of the new
system was "the concentration of business, industrial
and commercial, in the hands of a few, and the law of
competition between these," declared the process to be
"not only beneficial, but essential for the future progress of the race." [4] Carnegie's definition of progress is
conceptually not unlike Henry George's, but the term
has for him instead of George's intimations of disaster
the rich cluster of connotations generated by social
Darwinists and followers of Herbert Spencer: Carnegie insists that competition "insures the survival of
the fittest in every department."

II

I am concerned with how novelists translated into
imaginative terms the ideological debate that filled so
many thousands of pages during these strenuous years.

Fiction tells a story. It requires characters involved in situations; centrally, a protagonist performing a significant action. Fictional treatment of the emergence of industrial capitalism therefore focuses on the conception of the capitalist, the entrepreneur, as a type, and the way his deeds correspond to the functions imposed by his role. Mark Twain's Connecticut Yankee, Hank Morgan, is such a protagonist. His character and actions embody the writer's interpretation of the capitalist system. The story of Hank Morgan is drenched with the ideas put into circulation during the debate of the previous decade, and in a later chapter I shall examine the strands of ideology that entered into its composition. But these ideas need to be considered against a background of the attitudes prevalent in fictional treatment of social and economic issues when Mark Twain wrote *A Connecticut Yankee*. As it happens, during the same year in which that book was published two of his close literary associates brought out novels dealing with similar themes. In 1889 Charles Dudley Warner's *A Little Journey in the World* was published in book form by Harper's and William Dean Howells' *A Hazard of New Fortunes* ran as a serial in *Harper's Weekly*.

Warner was editor of the Hartford *Courant* and had some reputation as a critic. He had been a neighbor of Clemens' for almost twenty years in the comfortable and bookish Nook Farm community on the outskirts of the city. Soon after the Clemens family settled in

Nook Farm in 1872, Warner and Clemens had collaborated in writing a novel, *The Gilded Age,* which was one of the first efforts to give fictional treatment to post-Civil War economic and political turbulence. Warner's *A Little Journey* may profitably be viewed as a development of material he had contributed to this earlier joint effort. It is a very talky affair, with a garrulous first-person narrator resembling the writer. The principal events of the story are that Margaret Debree, a young woman with the usual equipment of beauty, charm, and cultivation, who represents the supreme achievement of the small New England city of Branton (that is, Hartford), refuses an offer of marriage from a highly moral visiting British nobleman and instead accepts Rodney Henderson, an urbane but unscrupulous lawyer of New England origin who has entered practice in New York. In association with "Uncle" Jerry Hollowell, Henderson has made a fortune through manipulation of railway grants and Congressmen. Margaret, drawn almost imperceptibly into the fashionable, frivolous world of her husband's associates, becomes a "dead soul," and presently dies. Henderson quickly marries one Carmen Eschelle, the beautiful and brilliant but cynical daughter of a man who (as the name suggests) represents the self-made new-rich of the metropolis.

This fable sets forth the destruction of the values of preindustrial New England by the expanding capitalism of the post-Civil War period—the world repre-

a collab.

sented at a more primitive stage of its development in *The Gilded Age*. Warner avoids the confusion of the earlier collaborative novel by a drastic simplification of plot, sacrificing in the process the variety and scope —and the humor—that have kept *The Gilded Age* alive despite its ramshackle structure. Margaret Debree is an almost allegorical embodiment of the simplicity, moral earnestness, and refinement in the name of which Warner passes judgment on shady big business and new-rich society. She bears a striking resemblance to Alice Montague, a character Warner had contributed to *The Gilded Age*, and the village of Fallkill in that novel has the moral tone that Warner attributes to Branton in *A Little Journey*. Indeed, both Fallkill and Branton are described by means of a quasi-pastoral cluster of images that recurs in many nineteenth-century novels by New England writers. The Montagues are moral paragons. They are, inevitably, descended from seventeenth-century English immigrants to Massachusetts Bay.

> With character compacted by the rigid Puritan discipline of more than two centuries, they had retained its strength and purity and thrown off its narrowness, and were now blossoming under the generous modern influences.

The family inhabits "a plain, roomy house, capable of extending to many guests an unpretending hospitality," which stands "alone with ample fields about it, . . . and on the west commanded a view of a pretty little

13

lake with gentle slopes and nodding groves." The
Montagues' economic basis is the more worthy of notice because Warner is so vague about it. Squire Montague has retired from the practice of law. We are told
nothing further about the source of his income except
that,

> Having only riches enough to be able to gratify reason-
> able desires, and yet make their gratifications always a
> novelty and a pleasure, the family occupied that just
> mean in life which is so rarely attained, and still more
> rarely enjoyed without discontent.

The "just mean" appropriate to a New England village implies a considerable degree of comfort, but
above all an imposing atmosphere of culture:

> Every room had its book-cases or book-shelves, and was
> more or less a library; upon every table was liable to be
> a litter of new books, fresh periodicals, and daily news-
> papers. There were plants in the sunny windows and
> some choice engravings on the walls, with bits of color
> in oil or water-colors; the piano was sure to be open and
> strewn with music; and there were photographs and
> little souvenirs here and there of foreign travel. . . .
> The life of the world flowed freely into this hospitable
> house, and there was always so much talk there of the
> news of the day, of the new books and of authors, of
> Boston radicalism and New York civilization, and the
> virtue of Congress, that small gossip stood a very poor
> chance.[5]

This is the fragile flower that the new forces of the Gilded Age threaten to destroy. Anglo-Saxon New England, left behind in the economic expansion that has established an axis connecting New York and Washington with the West, stands for a system of values that is supported by a secularized religion of culture. In a word, the Montague household embodies the genteel tradition.

III

Warner was unable to bring Fallkill and the Montagues into relation with any of the several lines of plot in *The Gilded Age;* poor Alice could not even be provided with a husband. In *A Little Journey* he has another try. He builds his entire plot around the marriage of Margaret Debree to a representative of the great world of high finance and sinister political maneuvers. This plan presented difficulties because it was hardly conceivable that a fastidious young heroine could be attracted by a typical railroad wrecker and manipulator of Congressional committees. Warner therefore splits the role of capitalist in two. The observed reality is represented by Hollowell, a vulgar but highly successful political and financial operator from the West. A plausible husband for Margaret is provided by reworking Henry Brierly, a recent graduate of Yale depicted in *The Gilded Age* as an apt pupil of the big businessmen and speculators who were the literary ancestors of

15

Jerry Hollowell. Rodney Henderson, Margaret Debree's suitor and eventually her husband in *A Little
Journey*, is also a native of New England and a college
graduate. But he is somewhat older and much more
forceful than Henry Brierly; he is already beginning to
be recognized as one of the coming men in New York
and Washington. At the same time, he is a collector of
first editions and paintings. He is presented as an at-
tentive and at least half-sincere lover. Even so, Warner
is reluctant to admit that a true daughter of the Puri-
tans might fall in love with a man whose moral stan-
dards allow him to succeed in the world of high finance.
Margaret's susceptibility to the attraction of Henderson has to be accounted for by giving her a French ancestor, an officer of Rochambeau's fleet who married
Margaret's great-grandmother.

These desperate expedients deserve attention only
because they reveal so transparently the problem that
Warner faced in constructing his story. Lacking con-
fidence that his plot can convey his meaning, he uses
the first-person narrator to make clear the contrast between the values of Branton and those of New York
and Washington. The narrator, named Fairchild, reports the prolonged discussions of Margaret and her
career in what he calls "our little parliament" back in
Branton. Like the Montague household, the Branton
circle stands for the highest moral and esthetic ideals:
there are the same books and magazines always in evidence, the same assumption of a decorous though not

16

fervent religious commitment. According to Fairchild, "the object in modern life is the cultivation of the mind, the elevation of women, and men also, in intellectual life." [6]

Now, however, Warner gives more attention to the economic basis for the good life that is lived in the parlors and on the verandas of Branton. One passage of the narrator's philosophizing is worth quoting despite its wordiness:

> In that June there were vexatious strikes in various parts of the country, formidable combinations of laboring-men, demonstrations of trades-unions, and the exhibition of a spirit that sharply called attention to the unequal distribution of wealth. The discontent was attributed in some quarters to the exhibition of extreme luxury and reckless living by those who had been fortunate. It was even said that the strikes, unreasonable and futile as they were, and most injurious to those who indulged in them, were indirectly caused by the railway manipulation, in the attempt not only to crush out competition, but to exact excessive revenues on fictitious values. Resistance to this could be shown to be blind, and the strikers technically in the wrong, yet the impression gained ground that there was something monstrously wrong in the way great fortunes were accumulated, in total disregard of individual rights, and in a materialistic spirit that did not take into account ordinary humanity.

"Ordinary humanity," it appears, is not the workers but the members of the little parliament—in effect,

Warner and the Nook Farm community. Fairchild
continues:

> For it was not alone the laboring class that was discon-
> tented, but all over the country those who lived upon
> small invested savings, widows and minors, found their
> income imperilled by the trickery of rival operators and
> speculators in railways and securities, who treated the
> little private accumulations as mere counters in the
> games they were playing. The loss of dividends to them
> was poorly compensated by reflections upon the devel-
> opment of the country, and the advantage to trade of
> great consolidations, which inured to the benefit of half
> a dozen insolent men.[7]

This is the language of a newspaper editorial. But
Warner gradually gets around to making his point in
terms of plot:

> In discussing these things in our little parliament [says
> Fairchild] we were not altogether unprejudiced, it must
> be confessed. For, to say nothing of interests of Mr. Mor-
> gan and my own, which seemed in some danger of dis-
> appearing for the "public good" [he has mentioned
> earlier an investment of his in a western railroad], Mrs.
> Fletcher's little fortune was nearly all invested in that
> sound "rock-bed" railway in the South-west that Mr.
> Jerry Hollowell had recently taken under his paternal
> care.[8]

The refinement of the Branton circle, then, is supported by investments in railway securities; the little

parliament is a rentier class. I do not intend to reduce the crisis of values to an issue of dollars and cents, but rather to suggest that Warner is speaking for a class which having in earlier generations dominated New England and the nation was now being shoved aside by the new "democratic plutocracy." [9] This historical change did not in itself invalidate the ethical or esthetic principles of the displaced class but it did throw into relief the usually unstated social-economic premises upon which conventional notions of refinement and cultivation rested. These notions were appropriate to people of hereditary status and a considerable amount of leisure.

Warner's phrase "democratic plutocracy" calls attention to essentially the same paradox with which Henry Adams was also wrestling in the 1880's as he composed his great history. Good or bad, valid or invalid, the genteel notion of ideality was class-bound, and could not survive the upheaval in American society caused by the industrialization that gained momentum during the middle decades of the century. The new captains of industry and manipulators of Congress had neither taste nor morals of their own to offer, but little was gained by genteel protests which merely called attention to the fact that the descendants of a preindustrial aristocracy had been jostled from control of the economy. The task that faced the writers of the post-Civil War period was the discovery or the construction of a new system of values taking into account the

19

new conditions. Mark Twain tried to do this in *A Connecticut Yankee*. Although he did not succeed fully in his undertaking, the fact that he embarked on it reveals the intuitive recognition of central issues and the courage that make him a serious writer—just as the lack of these qualities makes Warner a minor and properly forgotten figure.

IV

In *A Hazard of New Fortunes* Howells also attempted to deal with the moral questions raised by industrialization. This novel has the same general theme as Warner's *A Little Journey:* an evaluation of the "economic chance-world" [10] represented by New York and the new type of entrepreneur, from the perspective of a traditional system of values identified with New England. But in planning what Howells later called "the largest canvas I had yet allowed myself," "the most vital of my fictions," [11] he wisely abandoned the effort to state large social-economic-moral issues by means of a love story. He brings about the confrontation between New England morality and the world of Gilded-Age economics by viewing his materials through the eyes of Basil and Isabel March, the couple familiar to readers of his earlier books as fictionalized portraits of Howells himself and his wife. Instead of having to represent a marriage between a New England girl and a capitalist railway wrecker, Howells brings March into contact with the representative new millionaire, Jacob Dryfoos, by making him editor of a magazine that Dryfoos is financing in order to provide an occupation for his son Conrad. Jacob Dryfoos does not have to be subjected to cosmetic treatment as a prospective husband for a genteel heroine, and can therefore be endowed with all the vulgarity and hardness that Howells considered characteristic of the emergent economic rulers of America.

The over-all strategy of *A Hazard* is clearly superior to that of *A Little Journey*. A comparison of the two novels is instructive in other ways as well. For example, because Howells is not so fully identified with the Marches as Warner is with the "little parliament" in Branton, he can handle conventional New England attitudes with greater objectivity. The Marches represent Boston, but not Brahmin Boston. Isabel is a native of the city, a Bostonian "of great intensity both by birth and conviction," [12] and Basil, although he is like Howells a Westerner by origin, has lived there for twenty-five years before taking his new position in New York. Isabel March has what Howells and her husband regard with some detachment as a strain of "ancestral Puritanism." [13] The New England tradition is thus firmly planted in the story. Basil more than half shares his wife's attitudes, but Howells provides himself with a plausible means of criticizing them. Basil is ironically aware of his wife's implicit belief in the supreme merits of Boston culture: he is amused when she

21

says they cannot move to New York because she has just succeeded in getting their son and daughter into the Friday Afternoon Dancing Class. And in a moment of emotional disturbance Basil can even call the modest, sheltered refinement of their life in Boston a "death-in-life." [14]

Howells has a perspective on New England gentility that Warner never attained. The treatment of religion in the two novels shows a similar contrast. Warner's Branton moralists take churchgoing and mild philanthropies like the support of mission-schools among the poor as a matter of course, without showing an interest in theology or regarding religion as an urgent matter. The Marches have a comparable attitude. They attend services in various churches as a part of their systematic sight-seeing in New York but their sedate Unitarianism is not important for them. On the other hand, Howells places great emphasis on a Christian Socialism that is Episcopalian and High-Church: Conrad Dryfoos works assiduously in an Episcopal settlement house, and Margaret Vance, the wealthy young woman of high social standing with whom Conrad is chastely in love, is seen at the end of the novel in the garb of a religious order. In ascribing religion as a vital force to New York Episcopalians rather than to New England, Howells challenges the long-standing claim of that region to be the custodian of values for the nation.

The kind of unconscious self-righteousness that Warner shares with his Branton characters is subjected to further destructive criticism in Howells' novel. The little parliament enjoys a rather artificial immunity from the turmoils and temptations of the world that Margaret enters when she marries Rodney Henderson. On Warner's showing, virtue is distributed according to a vaguely pastoral pattern. It thrives in Branton but apparently nowhere else except among the English nobility; it withers in New York, Washington, and the summer colony of wealthy New Yorkers at Newport. By plunging the Marches physically into New York, by engaging them through March's job at least marginally in the great noisy system, Howells forces upon them a partial recognition of their "complicity" in the whole society. Basil discovers that the mentor of his youth, a German radical named Lindau, has chosen to live in a hideous slum because otherwise he feels himself to be in danger of forgetting the poor. Howells' own conscience is haunted by the vast poverty of the metropolis, for which he believes "comfortable people" are in some sense responsible.[15] When he first exposes March to the lower East Side, he holds him up for satire because of his lack of human sympathy with the dirty, swarming thousands in the streets. In the course of the story March meditates on the challenge of the slums, but Howells indicts the New England tradition by showing Basil and his wife to be no more than bothered and puzzled by this ugly stain on society.

The passionate concern that Howells could not plausibly ascribe to March finds expression in Conrad

Dryfoos, who literally dedicates his life to deeds of charity. Howells' bad conscience is much more disturbing than Warner's mild uneasiness over the problems of the new capitalism. Warner's case against the ruthless financiers consists in the demonstration that railway wrecking wipes out the small investments of middle-class residents of Branton. But Howells makes the New York slums into a vivid symbol of what is wrong with modern industrial society. The decorous mission-school teaching of Margaret Debree stands in significant contrast to the total commitment of Conrad and Margaret Vance.

V

Howells' deeper involvement in social issues appears also in his presentation of a wide variety of economic and political doctrines. The older aristocratic point of view is expounded by a rather stereotyped Southerner, Colonel Woodburn, who advocates a humane paternalism based on slavery as the only way to compel employers to accept responsibility for the welfare of the workers. The Colonel's feudalism is more extreme than any doctrine ever advocated in this country outside the South, but it does remind the reader of what had been lost when the last vestiges of the old ideal of a responsible aristocracy—as depicted for example by James Fenimore Cooper—were swept aside by the free-contractual capitalism of the post-Civil War period.

Poverty of the sort Howells brooded over in New York in the 1880's could not exist in the society imagined either by Cooper or by Colonel Woodburn; and this fact seemed of serious consequence to Howells, however archaic the feudal ideal might be.

Howells was more strongly drawn to the quasi-Marxist socialism of Lindau. He calls attention to how much the reactionary Woodburn and the radical Lindau have in common. At the very least, both of them have a scrupulous moral code which cannot tolerate the ruthlessness of Dryfoos. Lindau is a more plausible character than Woodburn in New York of the 1880's, for revolutionary socialism with a background in German Marxism was one of the strands in the public debate of the period. Howells was thinking also of the Chicago anarchists who had been active in the Haymarket disturbances of 1886, and whose conviction and execution on trumped-up charges had only recently shocked him into full awareness that class warfare was more than a metaphor in American industrial society. Howells had been one of the few prominent writers who denounced the violation of legality in the treatment of the anarchists. He was convinced—as recent historians have also been—that they were not responsible for setting off the bomb that killed seven policemen at the height of the rioting. But he had a horror of violence, and although he came to consider himself a socialist, he could not accept the implications of a revolutionary doctrine.

25

In *A Traveler from Altruria*, the Utopian romance Howells would write four years later, he would suggest, as did the followers of Edward Bellamy, that the people could take over the ownership of all means of production without violence, merely by voting in an election. Basil March, for all his admiration of Lindau, says explicitly at the end of the novel that Lindau died in a bad cause because he was inciting members of the streetcar workers' union to resist the police who were protecting strikebreakers.[16]

Nevertheless, in showing even a limited sympathy with Lindau's outright repudiation of capitalism Howells takes a position remote from Warner's mildly conventional protest against irresponsible financiers. Howells has no reservations about Conrad Dryfoos' Christian Socialism, and he notes that Conrad agrees in considerable part with Lindau's position, on scriptural grounds: "How hardly shall they that have riches enter into the kingdom of God." [17] Since Howells repudiated violent revolution and wavered in his belief that socialism could be achieved without violence, he was impelled toward a half-masochistic identification with Conrad's martyrdom. Conrad's way of life does not suggest how to eliminate poverty so much as it presents an almost ritual procedure by which a man might rid himself of the intolerable burden of guilt that the poverty of the slums places on him. In other words, the position is more Christian than socialist. Basil March reaches the conclusion (which Howells evidently shares) that when Conrad was accidentally shot while he was trying to persuade the strikers not to resort to violence, he "had some business there: it was his business to suffer there for the sins of others." [18] Yet even this is not, for Howells, an ultimately satisfactory conclusion. He could not find in himself the vocation of sainthood that he admired in Conrad; he did not have the religious faith which alone could give meaning to martyrdom. Furthermore, Howells' literary theory obliged him to regard Basil's moment of exaltation as an outburst of romanticism. Basil soon returns to the realistic level of common sense. When his wife reminds him that "Christ came into the world to teach us how to live rightly in it, too," he does not disagree, but retreats into a mild jest.[19]

Yet Howells' inability to share Conrad's heroic unworldliness does not mean that he accepts the premises of the new capitalism. His depiction of Jacob Dryfoos implies that the vast fortunes created by post-Civil War economic development were intrinsically wicked, that no man could become a millionaire honestly. Howells knows nothing and cares nothing about the details of large-scale financial or industrial operations. In this respect he is more naïve than Warner, who at least explains to the reader how Jerry Hollowell and Rodney Henderson enrich themselves by seizing control of a railroad in the Southwest. Howells' economic doctrine is based on the deeply-rooted genteel revulsion against speculation, the inveterate conviction that wealth rapidly gained is by definition immoral. The early stages of Dryfoos' financial career are rendered in some detail. A solid farmer in Indiana, he is suddenly uprooted from a sober life of hard work and thrift by the discovery of natural gas on his land. With the impetus of the local boom set off by the discovery, Dryfoos embarks on land speculation and real-estate developments. But from the moment when he has accumulated enough capital to move to New York and set himself up as a big operator in the stock market, his business activities disappear from the reader's view. Howells moralizes about the career instead of presenting it in novelistic terms:

His [Dryfoos'] moral decay began with his perception of the opportunity of making money quickly and abundantly, which offered itself to him after he sold his farm. . . . He devolved upon a meaner ideal than that of conservative good citizenship, which had been his chief moral experience: the money he had already made without effort and without merit bred its unholy self-love in him; he began to honor money, especially money that had been won suddenly and in large sums; for money that had been earned painfully, slowly, and in little amounts, he had only pity and contempt. . . . He came where he could watch his money breed more money, and bring greater increase of its kind in an hour of luck than the toil of hundreds of men could earn in a year.[20]

This schematic account of how Dryfoos became a millionaire stands in the novel as the type of large-scale economic activity. Howells, like Warner, does not recognize the productive capacity of industry; the new capitalism is for him exclusively a matter of buying and selling commodities and securities. Since he shows no awareness of the role of technology in American economic development, he regards the new fortunes of the post-Civil War decades as the result of successful gambling. In speaking of Dryfoos' operations he repeatedly uses the word "luck." [21] He takes it for granted that the businessman's activities are sterile and indeed criminal. Furthermore, by a process of inference that seems to lie below conscious analysis, Howells relates the poverty of the slums to the wicked gambling of the rich. What they win without labor is taken away from the helpless poor, and their guilt consists not only in their violation of the traditional doctrines of patient labor and steady frugality but in the sufferings of those from whom their wealth is stolen. Dryfoos' dedication to luck means, inevitably, that he comes to despise "intellectual ability." Basil asserts that he has "undergone a moral deterioration, an atrophy of the generous instincts." "He has sharpened," continues Basil, "but he has narrowed; his sagacity has turned into suspicion, his caution to meanness, his courage to ferocity." [22]

VI

In a series of conversations between Basil and Isabel March toward the end of the novel, Howells tries to bring the sprawling narrative into focus about the problem of order in the microcosm of New York to which the Marches have been so abundantly exposed. On one occasion Basil declares:

"It ought to be a law as inflexible in human affairs as the order of day and night in the physical world that if a man will work he shall both rest and eat, and shall not be harassed with any question as to how his repose and his provision shall come. Nothing less ideal than this satisfies the reason. But in our state of things no one is secure of this. No one is sure of finding work; no one is sure of not losing it. . . . and so we go on, pushing and pulling, climbing and crawling, thrusting aside and trampling underfoot; lying, cheating, stealing; and when we get to the end, covered with blood and dirt and sin and shame, and look back over the way we've come to a palace of our own, or the poor-house, which is about the only possession we can claim in common with our brother-men, I don't think the retrospect can be pleasing." [23]

Basil had meditated upon the problem early in the story, as he observed a New York slum. Howells' analysis of his impressions is remarkably obscure, but the more interesting on that account:

Accident and then exigency seemed the forces at work to this extraordinary effect; the play of energies as free and planless as those that force the forest from the soil to the sky; and then the fierce struggle for survival, with the stronger life persisting over the deformity, the mutilation, the destruction, the decay of the weaker. The whole at moments seemed to him lawless, godless; the absence of intelligent, comprehensive purpose in the huge disorder, and the violent struggle to subordinate the result to the greater good, penetrated with its dumb appeal the consciousness of a man who had always been too self-enwrapped to perceive the chaos to which the individual selfishness must always lead.[24]

What agent is supposed to be struggling to achieve the greater good? Howells' nearest approach to an answer is probably contained in March's final reflection upon the elder Dryfoos' helpless remorse over having quarreled with his son just before Conrad's death:

He thought how we never can atone for the wrong we do; . . . and yet we can put our evil from us with penitence; and somehow, somewhere, the order of loving kindness, which our passion or our wilfulness has disturbed, will be restored.[25]

VII

After one of Basil March's efforts to "philosophize" Dryfoos he had concluded ruefully that "such a man and his experience are the ideal and ambition of most

Americans." [26] Through much of the novel Howells seems to share Basil's opinion: Dryfoos is a full-scale effort to depict a typical Gilded Age capitalist. But in Fulkerson, the business manager of *Every Other Week*, the magazine Basil edits and Dryfoos finances, he presents an even more fully developed portrait of a quite different kind of businessman. Perhaps we may say that Dryfoos is the inner-directed type characteristic of the heroic age of American capitalism, whereas Fulkerson foreshadows the other-directed personality that David Riesman tells us has become prevalent in the twentieth century. Fulkerson's most striking trait is an invincible cheerfulness: Howells says, "He was one of those Americans whose habitual conception of life is unalloyed prosperity. When any experience or observation of his went counter to it he suffered something like physical pain." [27] Fulkerson shows great energy in carrying out his schemes. Picking up a casual suggestion made by March about the possibility of running a magazine on the co-operative principle, he singlehandedly brings the journal into being and into successful operation. Yet he instinctively dislikes conflict; he wants to make himself agreeable. In this effort he is remarkably successful. He persuades not only March, but the prickly artist Beaton to join the enterprise; and even Mrs. March is enchanted with him.

Fulkerson's gift for interpersonal relations is not based on hypocrisy, for he simply has no awkward opinions of his own; he takes over his attitudes from his associates. Thus he is capable of relating with gusto how Dryfoos intimidated the workers on his gas wells by bringing in strikebreakers protected by armed Pinkerton agents. Yet he is astonished and distressed by Lindau's outrage over the incident. When Dryfoos orders March to discharge Lindau from his position of translator for the magazine, Fulkerson assumes March will obey, but after discussing the matter with the Woodburns he ends up supporting March. In an earlier scene he proposes to March that the first number of the magazine should include "a good, swinging attack" on the work of an advanced-guard novelist whom Fulkerson admires. "What an immoral little wretch you are, Fulkerson!" says the editor with a laugh. March is half in earnest but Fulkerson is unperturbed: ". . . when it comes to that first number, I'd offer up anybody" is his line.[28] He wants publicity at any cost, and on a later occasion March calls him "a pure advertising essence."[29] He is clearly a pioneer manipulator of what would come to be known as the mass media.

Fulkerson is unlike Dryfoos not only in his geniality and gregariousness but also in his quick if shallow intelligence and his easy familiarity with as much literature and art as are involved in the publishing business. He is aware of the drawings in current Spanish magazines and of the fact that "those French fellows" gave Daudet thirty-five thousand dollars to write a novel for use with illustrations printed by a new process. His conversation is sprinkled with half-punning literary al-

33

lusions and he is even capable of throwing in a tag from Goethe: "What we want to do is to work the *ewig Weibliche* in this concern." [30]

Fulkerson is much more nearly alive as a character than is Dryfoos, who seems overschematic in conception. The reason is almost certainly that Howells' prolonged exposure to the world of magazine publishing gave him an authority in rendering journalists and editors that he could never achieve in writing about new-rich millionaires. How much opportunity could he have had to observe Wall Street operators at close range? A further advantage Howells enjoyed in presenting Fulkerson was the novelist's genuine gift for humor—a resource that is never brought to bear on Dryfoos. Fulkerson is amusing in a special way. He is glib and as Howells says, slangy. He employs a consciously exaggerated vernacular but flavors it with a burlesque of exalted diction. The reader can hardly help wondering whether Fulkerson is not a lineal descendant of Beriah Sellers, the irrepressible speculator that Mark Twain had depicted in *The Gilded Age*. Sellers of course had neither Fulkerson's ironic manner nor his shrewdness in practical matters. But Fulkerson's imagination has at least some of Sellers' comic amplitude, and he closely resembles the Colonel in the way his promoter's enthusiasm springs from an underlying good will and even a kind of innocence.

A Hazard of New Fortunes presents then two disparate and even contradictory renderings of the busi-

34

nessman as a type: the hard, narrow Dryfoos, who expresses Howells' humanitarian and theoretical hostility toward American capitalism as a system; and Fulkerson, a shallow but inoffensive and likable character who seems to be based on the novelist's first-hand observation of the businessmen he knew best—the inventive pioneers who brought into being that characteristic American institution of the later nineteenth century, the literary magazine aimed at a large national audience. Whatever Fulkerson may owe to Colonel Sellers, he shows unmistakable similarities to another character created by Mark Twain. He has much in common with Hank Morgan, the energetic promoter with an instinct for publicity stunts who sets about bringing King Arthur's Britain up to date.

[handwritten at top:] Initially over Tw's. idea to use the progress of 19th + tech. of realism to discredit 6th / Romantic Ideals

2. FROM BURLESQUE TO NIGHTMARE:

The Genesis of a Fable

[handwritten marginalia:] *time jumps no longer a convenient stage setting technique for Twis tale of contrasts & progress*

I

[handwritten left margin: X]

If one looks at *A Connecticut Yankee* against the background provided by Warner's *A Little Journey in the World* and Howells' *A Hazard of New Fortunes*, the similarities and differences are almost equally impressive. All three novels deal with the new industrial capitalism that had come into existence so suddenly during the Gilded Age. It is true that Mark Twain professes to be rehearsing a dream about a far-away country, the Britain of King Arthur and his Round Table. But this medieval setting is obviously not meant to represent any actual place or time. It is a backdrop designed to allow a nineteenth-century American industrial genius to show what he can do with an underdeveloped country. Mark Twain's subject is the same as Warner's and Howells': the transformation of men and institutions by rapid industrial development. And all three novelists take it for granted that this transformation is the central fact of modern life.

[handwritten left margin: X initially]

[handwritten at bottom:] * By the novel's close time-jumping episodes have taken on a greater significance — no longer peripheral convenient stage-setting tech — the dislocation becomes an essential part of the novels trauma of loss & dislocation

Link to why Tw.
chose fantasy mode :- see :- Mech. Accents

The contrast between Mark Twain's story and the other two does not lie in differences of setting, but in the diametrically opposed points of view from which the problems of industrialization are surveyed. Warner and Howells share a common hostility to the new capitalists, represented by Rodney Henderson, Jerry Hollowell, and Jacob Dryfoos. They both view such men as a menace to traditional values, and in portraying them imply that the whole capitalist system is tainted, that the entrepreneur's motives are basically selfish and his activities parasitic if not actually criminal. Mark Twain, on the other hand, chooses to identify himself with the businessman. Hank Morgan is an engineer and executive who undertakes the task of bringing about an industrial revolution in Arthur's kingdom. Ostensibly this program has Mark Twain's complete approval: the Yankee is the standard-bearer of progress, determined to overthrow feudal tyranny and to bring such basic decencies as food, clothing, shelter, and education to the impoverished and exploited common people of Britain. Mark Twain's assumptions about industrialization and capitalism thus seem—offhand, at least —exactly the opposite of Warner's and Howells'.

A Connecticut Yankee was the first literary effort of any consequence to treat the entrepreneur sympathetically. There had of course been earlier works that took the side of the businessman, from Washington Irving's brief but laudatory references to John Jacob Astor in Astoria (1836) to Horatio Alger's rags-to-riches stories

37

Note if at beginning :- Tw's fantastic event of Yankee miraculously awakening in 6th was a convenient plot-setting up / artificial technique used to conveniently setup his stage ←

that began to appear in the 1860's. But none of these books can be said to come to grips with the issue. They are quite naïve in their conception of economic processes. Alger, for example, although he would never have thought of raising doubts about the existing economic system, was as fully convinced as Howells that success in business is mainly a matter of luck. The way to wealth is usually opened up for his Tattered Toms by improbable coincidences: they rescue the boss's daughter from a runaway horse, receive an unexpected inheritance, and so on. *The Bread Winners*, a novel published in 1883 by Mark Twain's friend John Hay, is hardly more sophisticated in its treatment of economic problems. Hay devotes most of his energies to vilifying the "walking delegate" or union organizer who stirs up discontent in well-treated and previously happy laborers.

These pro-capitalist stories are written from a genteel point of view. They show no more awareness than does Warner that the traditional value system is becoming irrelevant. They merely attempt to substitute the new capitalist for the country gentleman that James Fenimore Cooper had placed in control of his ideal society, without really recognizing the transition from an agrarian to an industrial economic system. The novelty of Mark Twain's approach to his materials lies in his deliberate abandonment of the genteel perspective. Hank Morgan belongs to the working class; he has risen from the ranks of workers to the position of superintendent in the Colt arms factory in Hartford. The controlling item in the account he gives of himself at the outset of his narrative is that he is "practical" and "nearly barren of sentiment . . . —or poetry, in other words." [1] Lacking any pretensions to refinement, he can avow his unabashed loyalty to the profit motive. At the same time the Yankee is practical in the sense that he can get things done. For the purposes of the fable, he is given the power to make any machine known to modern industry; he is a personification of technological skill and inventiveness. The nearest thing to poetry in him is what Mark Twain called his "circus side." [2] He has a flair for publicity. He delights in gaudy and vulgar display; he is constantly calling attention to himself and advertising his own accomplishments.

Despite the Yankee's antics and the side-splitting predicaments he falls into, his command of technology makes him at least potentially a hero of epic dimensions, a man with a world-historical mission. His plan of industrializing Arthur's Britain resembles Prometheus' defiance of the tyrannical gods for the sake of bringing to man the priceless gift of intellectual light and technological power. *A Connecticut Yankee* is thus not a mere tall tale but a philosophical fable which sets forth a theory of capitalism and an interpretation of the historical process that has brought it into being.[3]

& a value laden analogy

II

Howard Baetzhold has recently established the dates when the various parts of *A Connecticut Yankee* were written.[4] Mark Twain worked on the book over a period of almost five years from its first conception to its publication near the end of 1889. Since he did not systematically revise earlier chapters to bring them into accord with his changing conceptions of plot and character, the text as finally published resembles a geologist's stratigraphic series. A knowledge of the chronological order of the strata enables the reader to observe the first appearance and the subsequent evolution of ideas and themes which undergo drastic changes in meaning. In many passages elements representing earlier stages in Mark Twain's conception of the story are mingled with those representing later and incongruous developments in his thought.

Mr. Baetzhold distinguishes five stages in the composition of the book:

Stage 1. *December 1884:* A notebook entry recording a dream about the discomforts of wearing armor suggested by Mark Twain's reading in Malory's *Morte d'Arthur*.

Stage 2. *1885:* Random notebook entries that deal with incidents later incorporated in the story.

Stage 3. *Probably January-February 1886:* Composi-

40

tion of the prefatory "Word of Explanation" and Chapters I-III in approximately their final form.

Stage 4. *Summer 1887:* Composition of Chapters IV-XX (except Chapter X).

Stage 5. *July 1888-May 1889:* Composition of the remainder of the book—Chapters X and XXI-XLIV (with the two "Postscripts").

STAGE 1 (DECEMBER 1884)

The notebook entry concerning the dream suggested by the *Morte d'Arthur* is as follows:

Dream of being a knight errant in armor in the middle ages. Have the notions & habits of thought of the present day mixed with the necessities of that. No pockets in the armor. No way to manage certain requirements of nature. Can't scratch. Cold in the head—can't blow —can't get at handkerchief, can't use iron sleeve. Iron gets red hot in the sun—leaks in the rain, gets white with frost & freezes me solid in winter. Suffer from lice & fleas. Make disagreeable clatter when I enter church. Can't dress or undress myself. Always getting struck by lightning. Fall down, can't get up. See Morte d'Arthur.[5]

This dream would prove to have an almost inexhaustible store of meanings, but its presented surface is simple. It is the germ of a literary burlesque. Mark Twain had often practiced this mode. For example, in

41

*Important
- this clearly
changed*

1881 he had toyed with the notion of adding a book
salesman named Basil Stockmar to the cast of *Hamlet*.[6]
Like all burlesque the dream embodies an element of
hostility toward its target. It calls attention to the absurdity of the romantic aura surrounding knighthood
and chivalry. When Mark Twain imagines himself in
armor, he does not feel humiliated because he cannot
adapt himself to the strange costume, but assumes that
his "notions & habits of thought" are normal and rational, the wearing of armor eccentric or even idiotic.

In the background is the conviction that modern
civilization is in every way superior to that of the Middle Ages. Nevertheless, even in his dream Mark
Twain's imagination follows a pattern exemplified in
many of his earlier comic sketches. He makes himself
the butt of the joke. The man so uncomfortable in his
iron clothing is at the mercy of undignified animal necessities. In this respect the dream resembles the anec-
dote in *The Innocents Abroad* (Vol. I, Chap. XII)
in which the narrator is lured into the chair of a Parisian
barber who scrapes the skin off his face with a dull
razor, or the story of how the tenderfoot in *Roughing
It* (Vol. I, Chap. XXIV) is gulled into buying a "genuine Mexican plug" horse that runs away with him.

STAGE 2 (1885)

Within a few weeks the notebook presents another
entry not explicitly related to the original dream but

42

also placing modern men in a medieval setting, and evidently containing an idea for a story:

> Have a battle between modern army with gatling guns —(automatic) 600 shots a minute, with one pulling of the trigger, torpedos, balloons, 100-ton cannon, ironclad fleet &c & Prince de Joinville's Middle Age Crusaders.[7]

The amusing burlesque dream has become startlingly brutal. The Gatling guns probably influenced the later decision to make the nineteenth-century invader of Arthur's Britain foreman of the Colt arms factory in Hartford, for it was at this factory that Mark Twain had first seen a Gatling gun and had been allowed to fire it.[8] Eventually the Connecticut Yankee would slaughter a whole army of knights by means of a fearsome array of modern weapons, including thirteen Gatling guns.

Two other notebook entries throw light on the working of Mark Twain's mind in the early stages of the incubation of his plot. The terse phrase "Country placed under an interdict" shows that he had decided to bring his protagonist into conflict with the Church.[9] A longer entry mentions an Arthurian heroine for whom the protagonist yearns after he has been returned to the nineteenth century.[10]

link again to fantasy — a distancing technique — he used others

STAGE 3 (1886)

Mr. Baetzhold believes that between December 1885 and mid-February 1886 Mark Twain composed the introductory "Word of Explanation" and the first three chapters in substantially their final form. On 11 November 1886 he read these chapters in New York before a fashionable audience composed of members of the Military Service Institution (including General William T. Sherman), their wives, and guests, among whom was the General's brother, the millionaire Senator. He also read a part of what was to become Chapter VIII and sketched in briefly some of his ideas about the remainder of a book he said was still unwritten. Reports of the occasion in two New York newspapers—the *Herald* and the *Sun*—permit fairly complete reconstruction of what Mark Twain said. The reporter for the *Sun* evidently had access to the manuscript of the completed chapters; he quotes several paragraphs that differ hardly at all from the final text.

who Tw publ mem of

By this time the situation depicted in the original dream has begun to grow into a first-person narrative about the adventures of an American called Sir Robert Smith.[11] As the original dream indicates, this character is at bottom Mark Twain, but his opening description of himself shows the influence of two additional images: the traditional folk figure of the shrewd rustic Yankee—the cultural ancestor of Uncle Sam—and a

44

new type of industrial worker possessing the whole
range of modern technological knowledge and skills:

> I am an American. I was born and reared in Hartford, in
> the state of Connecticut—anyway, just over the river,
> in the country. So I am a Yankee of the Yankees—and
> practical; yes, and nearly barren of sentiment, I suppose
> —or poetry, in other words. My father was a black-
> smith, my uncle was a horsedoctor, and I was both,
> along at first. Then I went over to the great arms fac-
> tory and learned my real trade; learned all there was to
> it; learned to make everything: guns, revolvers, cannon,
> boilers, engines, all sorts of labor-saving machinery.
> Why, I could make anything a body wanted—anything
> in the world, it didn't make any difference what; and if
> there wasn't any quick new-fangled way to make a
> thing, I could invent one—and do it as easy as rolling off
> a log. I became head superintendent; had a couple of
> thousand men under me.[12]

The close relation between technology and weapons
here is understandable: it was armor that had symbol-
ized medieval culture in the original dream; Malory
devotes most of his pages to various forms of combat;
and Mark Twain had had the impulse to imagine what
modern weapons could do against those of the Middle
Ages. The Yankee's practicality and lack of esthetic
sensibility were familiar traits of the prevalent image of
the American male. Mark Twain had depicted the
type, for example, in *The Innocents Abroad*.

But what was the protagonist to do in Arthur's

45

realm? What was to be the action of the story? The most definite clue is the Yankee's statement that the people he observed at Arthur's court were so simple-minded he knew he could "boss the whole country inside of three months; for I judged I would have the start of the best-educated man in the kingdom by a matter of thirteen hundred years and upwards." [13] In other words, he intends to seek power, and he expects to achieve it by means of a superior "education" that has been gained in the Colt factory rather than in a college.

The report in the New York *Sun* of Mark Twain's comments about incidents to be included in chapters yet unwritten throws light on the Yankee's education:

> He took a contract from King Arthur to kill off, at one of the great tournaments, fifteen kings and many acres of hostile armored knights. When, lance in rest, they charged by squadrons upon him, he, behind the protection of a barbed wire fence charged with electricity, mowed them down with Gatling guns that he had made for the occasion. He found that the "education of the nineteenth century is plenty good enough capital to go into business in the sixth century with," and the next year he was running the kingdom all by himself on a moderate royalty of forty per cent.

This extraordinary tournament is not integrated with the other hints about the Yankee's actions; it seems to persist in the writer's mind obsessively rather than as part of a coherent plot. It would eventually be developed into the all-out battle that ends the Yankee's nar-

46

rative. At this stage, however, Mark Twain places more emphasis on his hero's plans for making money. The report in the *Sun* concludes:

> He spoiled the ogre business; cleared out the fuss and flummery of romance and put King Arthur's kingdom on a strictly business basis. Inside of three and a half years the improvement was complete. Cast-iron clothes had gone out of fashion. Sir Launcelot was running a kind of Louisiana lottery. The search for the Holy Grail had been given up for a hunt for the Northwest Passage. King Arthur's 140 illustrious Knights had turned themselves into a stock Board, and a seat at the Round Table was worth $30,000.[14]

This version of the story shows no interest in politics. The kingdom is an absolute monarchy, and Mark Twain assumes the political system will remain unchanged. The Yankee will exploit a grant of power from the King, attained somehow by means of his modern weapons, in order to make money for the King and himself. The members of the existing aristocracy are not attacked for their oppression of the common people, but are allowed to share in the profits of the Yankee's enterprise. To some extent the economic assumptions follow the outlines of eighteenth-century colonial capitalism; the mention of a Louisiana lottery seems to be a reference to John Law and the great monopolies established by French monarchs before the Revolution. Or Mark Twain may have in mind the operations of the British in India: the entrepreneur enters a society

47

at a low level of economic development, establishes his control by means of superiority in weapons and shrewd alliances with the native rulers, and puts things on a business basis. At the same time, the emphasis on a relatively simple kind of commercialism is an appropriate extension of the "cuteness," the petty shrewdness in trade, that was a recognized trait of the folklore Yankee peddler with his hard bargains and wooden nutmegs.[15]

To summarize: in the story as Mark Twain planned it in 1886 he had endowed the Yankee with technological skill but had not decided how to use it in the plot except in the manufacture of weapons. The hero is a businessman rather than an engineer or an industrialist. Political reform is not so much as mentioned. The story is still quite close in tone to the original dream—that is, to a comic burlesque of the *Morte d'Arthur*. The narrative plan Mark Twain had in mind was shaped by the general idea of a contrast between the remote, dreamlike, exalted tone of Malory's imaginary world and the bumptious vulgarity of an intruder from the nineteenth century—a figure not basically unlike the book salesman Mark Twain had introduced to the castle at Elsinore. This kind of burlesque, common in the work of Western humorists, was essentially irresponsible. The writer merely made a quick comic profit from the incongruity between "high" and "low." In the course of time Mark Twain would perceive deeper meanings in his contrast of civilizations, but in

1886 his protagonist was simply an operator who had stumbled on a good thing in the speculative line.

Yet Mark Twain was not fully identified with the Yankee thumbing his nose at chivalry, and by the same token was not wholly committed to the side of business as against feudalism. His attitudes wavered. When his old friend and mentor Mrs. Mary Fairbanks wrote him from Cleveland in some alarm over newspaper reports of the lecture before the Military Service Institution, he hastened to assure her that his book would not show irreverence toward Malory. The story "isn't a satire peculiarly," he declared, "it is more especially a *contrast*. It merely exhibits under high lights, the daily life of the time & that of to-day . . ." In a paragraph which at first glance seems disingenuous but which merely exaggerates a genuine facet of Mark Twain's attitude at that time, he assures her of his reverence for the priggish Arthurian world that Tennyson had taught Victorian readers to find in Malory:

Of course in my story I shall leave unsmirched & unbelittled the great & beautiful *characters* drawn by the master hand of old Malory . . . I shall hope that under my hand Sir Galahad will still remain the divinest spectre that one glimpses among the mists & twilights of Dreamland across the wastes of the centuries; & Arthur keep his sweetness & his purity, and Launcelot abide & continue "the kindest man that ever strake the sword," yet "the sternest knight to his mortal foe that ever put spear in the rest"; & I should grieve indeed if the final disruption of the Round Table, & the extinction of its old tender & gracious friendships, & that last battle—the Battle of the Broken Hearts, it might be called—should lose their pathos & their tears through my handling.[16]

In the chapters composed before this letter was written Mark Twain had satirized Arthur's court by joyous attention to the dogs fighting over bones tossed them by the feasting knights, and had remarked that "There did not seem to be brains enough in the entire nursery, so to speak, to bait a fish-hook with." [17] But he had not fully disengaged himself from conventional genteel attitudes toward Arthurian romance. He had asserted that "there was something very engaging about these great simple-hearted creatures, something attractive and lovable," and had paraded a highly reverent vocabulary in describing the "fine manliness," "loftiness and sweetness," "noble benignity and purity" and even "majesty and greatness" of King Arthur, Galahad, and Launcelot.[18] At this stage in his work he maintains a considerable degree of detachment in handling the contrast between civilizations. Although basically he is of course convinced that the nineteenth century is superior, he can perceive both the element of vulgarity in his modern protagonist and the element of nobility, if not of sophistication, in the knights. He is perceptibly ironic about the Yankee's brash proposal to put the kingdom on a business basis.

STAGE 4 (1887)

After Mark Twain had composed three chapters early
in 1886, he did not add substantially to the manuscript
of *A Connecticut Yankee* for more than a year. But in
the summer of 1887 he wrote sixteen additional chapters (IV-XX, excluding X, which was inserted later).
The new material consists of two sequences: Chapters
IV-IX, in which the Yankee rises to power as The
Boss, and Chapters XI-XX, in which the dream of
wearing armor is expanded into his excursion with the
Demoiselle Alisande la Carteloise (or "Sandy") to the
enchanted pigsty.

The Yank's "cuteness" figures prominently in his
seizure of power. He saves himself from being burned
at the stake by pretending that an eclipse of the sun is
caused by his magical powers, and extorts from the
King an agreement set forth in technical terms of commercial law: "You shall remain king over all your do-
minions, and receive all the glories and honors that
belong to the kingship; but you shall appoint me your
perpetual minister and executive, and give me for my
services one per cent of such actual increase of rev-
enue over and above its present amount as I may succeed in creating for the state." [19] The Yankee's demand
has been reduced to a more plausible figure from the
"moderate royalty of forty per cent" mentioned earlier, but he is still primarily out to make money for
himself. In Chapter IX, for example, when he is de-

51

scribing the expeditions that "went out holy grailing" every year, he adds: "There was worlds of reputation in it, but no money. Why, they actually wanted *me* to put in! Well, I should smile." [20] The deliberate contrast between the Yankee's philistine commercialism and the idealism of the Grail quest shows that Mark Twain still holds back from full identification with the narrator.

The predominance of economic motives in the Yankee at this stage is indicated by several of his comments about himself. For example, in Chapter VII he says:

> I saw that I was just another Robinson Crusoe cast away on an uninhabited island, with no society but some more or less tame animals, and if I wanted to make life bearable I must do as he did—invent, contrive, create, reorganize things; set brain and hand to work, and keep them busy. Well, that was in my line.[21]

In Chapter VIII he alludes to Horace Greeley's advice to young Americans on the make: "Look at the opportunities here for a man of knowledge, brains, pluck, and enterprise to sail in and grow up with the country." A few lines later the Yankee compares his plans to "Joseph's splendid financial ingenuities," which Mark Twain had earlier described rather flippantly as the first large-scale corner on the grain market.[22]

Overtly, Mark Twain still conceives of his protagonist as an organizer, a speculator, an entrepreneur, and assumes that he will enrich himself by exploiting the power he has gained through his claim to be a magician. The chapters written in 1887, however, contain some foreshadowing of the Yankee's later feats as an engineer and industrialist. In retaliation for Merlin's effort to have him executed, he decides to blow up the magician's tower. He remarks in an offhand manner that he and his assistant, the page Clarence, "clandestinely . . . made a few bushels of first-rate blasting powder, and I superintended my armorers while they constructed a lightningrod and some wires." To ignite his charges he depends on a thunderstorm that appears as fortuitously as the eclipse.[23]

The conception of the Yankee as a magician is new material but is left in a rudimentary state. Another theme first introduced in 1887, however, is developed at great length and with passionate energy. This is the polemic against feudal laws and institutions. Mark Twain launches his attack on medieval aristocracy by picking up an idea mentioned casually in his 1886 lecture—the Yankee's farcical sally to confront an ogre —and combining it with two other ideas from the notebooks: the original dream of wearing armor and the introduction of a heroine, whom the Yankee reluctantly accompanies to rescue forty-five princesses and noble ladies imprisoned by an ogre in an enchanted castle. The account of this adventure occupies ten chapters (XI-XX). By a brilliant inversion of the Don Quixote-Sancho Panza relationship it becomes the comic triumph of the book; the ironic conception of

53

the swine who must be called "my lady" and "your highness" is a crude but unforgettably vivid insult to European aristocracies. Yet in much of the sequence, Mark Twain relies on the rather unimaginative and far from comic device of having the travelers witness various atrocities perpetrated by the nobles upon the common people. On such occasions the Yankee becomes merely a passive observer or (as in the scenes in Morgan Le Fay's palace) a thin disguise for the author.

Mark Twain's identification of himself with the narrator at this stage of the book implies a kind of retroactive endorsement of the commercialism which had been subjected to ironic criticism in earlier chapters. But in proportion as the writer abandons his detachment and makes the Yankee into a mouthpiece for his own views, the protagonist ceases to be an entrepreneur in search of profit and becomes a humanitarian emancipator of the downtrodden peasants. Mark Twain's failure to undertake the revisions that would have been necessary to confer a consistent motivation on the Yankee left an element of obscurity in the narrative that puzzles the modern reader.

STAGE 5 (1888–89)

The chapters from XXI to the end, together with Chapter X, were written between July 1888 and the spring of 1889. Although Mark Twain did not put aside the manuscript for very long at any one time dur-

54

ing this period, Mr. Baetzhold has identified some brief interruptions. Nearly all of chapters XXI-XXXVI were written during the Clemens family's usual summer stay at Quarry Farm near Elmira, the home of Olivia Clemens' foster-sister Susan Crane and her husband Theodore. The material in these chapters includes the description of the band of pilgrims encountered by Hank Morgan and Sandy on their return from the pigsty; the Yankee's exploits in the Valley of Holiness; and the travels of the Yankee and the King through the countryside incognito.

Mark Twain's increasing identification with the Yankee, which becomes noticeable in the satiric parts of the chapters written in 1887, seems to have made him impatient with his hero's passive role. He begins to show an almost personal animosity toward the Yankee's rivals and enemies. The Valley of Holiness sequence, for example, reaches its climax in a contest between the Yankee and Merlin, who tries unsuccessfully to restore a holy well that has gone dry. The difficulty proves to be trivial: all that is needed is to repair a hole in the masonry lining which has been allowing the water to escape. But the Yankee seizes the opportunity to destroy the prestige of a competitor and solidify his own position as acknowledged Boss of the kingdom. He makes elaborate plans for dramatizing his feat before the multitude gathered in the Valley. He sends a messenger to his headquarters at Camelot with an order for some pipe, a hand pump, and a great quantity of fireworks. The pump will enable him to produce a stream of water outside the well-house at the moment when he utters a series of jaw-breaking pseudo-German incantations and sets off a display of rockets and Roman candles. It was apparently the provision of fireworks that made Mark Twain aware for the first time that he must pay some attention to the industrial plant needed by his hero. The requisition sent to Camelot implies the existence of a vast warehouse and a staff of trained assistants. He therefore paused to compose a summary chapter (X) for insertion much earlier in the story in order to account for the equipment that would be required in the industrialization of Arthurian society:

> In various quiet nooks and corners [says the narrator] I had the beginnings of all sorts of industries under way —nuclei of future vast factories, the iron and steel missionaries of my future civilization. In these were gathered together the brightest young minds I could find, and I kept agents out raking the country for more, all the time. I was training a crowd of ignorant folk into experts—experts in every sort of handiwork and scientific calling. These nurseries of mine went smoothly and privately along undisturbed in their obscure country retreats, for nobody was allowed to come into their precincts without a special permit—for I was afraid of the Church.[24]

The reference to the hostility of the Church points up the fact that Merlin is not clearly linked with either the Established Church or the monarchy in Arthur's kingdom; although there is one joking reference to wages paid him by the King, he seems on the whole to be self-employed. The Yankee's dazzling demonstration that his magic is more powerful than Merlin's does not, therefore, have a clear political significance, although it does show that the magic of technology is stronger than Merlin's empty magic of superstition. If the polemic against feudal tyranny was to be translated into terms of plot, the Yankee had to perform a more significant action. Mark Twain was evidently unable for some time to hit upon a plot device that would serve this purpose. While he and the King, in disguise, are having dinner at the house of a charcoal burner, the Yankee expounds for his peasant auditors ideas about currency inflation and the protective tariff representing the Democratic position during Grover Cleveland's campaign for the presidency in 1888.[25] But the effort at rational enlightenment of the common people leads only to an undignified brawl. Mark Twain falls back upon further documentation of social and legal abuses in Arthurian Britain by causing the Yankee and King to be seized as runaway slaves and added to the coffle of a trader who takes them to London. But after three or four additional chapters of this material the polemic against feudalism begins to yield diminishing returns, and the narrative veers toward a pure cloak-and-dagger adventure-story pattern. At the end of the summer of 1888 he had completed present Chapter XXXVIII, leaving the Yankee and the King in London in chains and about to be executed along with the other slaves of the murdered trader. The tank of inspiration —to use Mark Twain's metaphor for his spasmodic method of composition—had obviously been emptied. He was in a cul-de-sac from which he could see no way to extricate himself. None of the major issues of the story was resolved and he was apparently at a loss how to resolve them.

Part of the difficulty with the story must have been due to the unhappy state of Mark Twain's personal affairs. His publishing company was in trouble—as he believed, because of the mismanagement of his nephew Charles L. Webster, but in reality because he was constantly draining capital out of it to meet the inordinate expense of perfecting a pilot model of the typesetter that was being constructed in the Pratt-Whitney works in Hartford under the direction of the inventor Paige. During the latter part of 1888 the machine was costing Clemens some three thousand dollars a month, and the family felt so short of money that Jean Clemens—aged eight—told a maid she must not ask for a box of blacking for the children's shoes.[26] Yet the money had to be found if everything already invested in the machine was not to be lost. In the late summer Theodore Crane suffered a paralytic stroke. The Clemenses delayed their return to Hartford so that Livy might help his wife nurse him, and Crane was later brought to the Clemens house in Hartford for medical treatment. Livy's health, never robust, was impaired by the physical and emotional strain of her duties as nurse and hostess. She contracted a disease of the eyes that for weeks on end prevented her from reading. These and other misfortunes darkened the Clemens household throughout the rest of the winter.

Nevertheless, Mark Twain worked, when he could, at his writing; it was a means of escape for him. While the family were settling themselves back into the Hartford house at the beginning of October, he reported to his brother-in-law that he had taken over an upstairs room of the near-by Twichell house as a study, and had written 80 pages in five days despite the noise of carpenters constructing a new ceiling in the room below: the blows of the hammers made his feet tingle.[27] He had more than one reason for being eager to finish *A Connecticut Yankee*. The publishing house needed a salable book to bring out. Mark Twain himself, who had produced no work of any consequence since the publication of *Adventures of Huckleberry Finn* almost four years earlier, was anxious about his hold on his audience and perhaps even assailed by fears that his creative powers were exhausted.[28] He had conceived the irrational notion that there was some link between the book and the typesetting machine. He wanted to have both completed on the same day, which at one time he mistakenly thought might be October 22, 1888. As James M. Cox has suggested, there are even hints that he sometimes imagined an occult analogy between himself and the typesetter—both of them being near-miraculous mechanisms for producing words. It is clear that he not only personified the machine but projected much of his frustration and anxiety into it, so that it became for him alternately a "sublime magician" and a "cunning devil." [29] Yet another link of analogy established by his overwrought imagination during this period of strain connected the typesetter with the hidden system of factories that Hank Morgan had created and that he intended to unveil suddenly before an astonished nation. Early in January 1889, still hoping desperately for the completion of the machine, Clemens wrote to his brother: "In two or three weeks we shall work the stiffness out of her joints and have her performing as smoothly and softly as human muscles, and then we shall speak out the big secret and let the world come and gaze." [30] Yet the machine continued to disappoint him. There was always some further expensive adjustment to be made, and it would in fact prove in the end a failure, after he had sunk perhaps two hundred thousand dollars in it.

It is no doubt impossible to determine what effect these anxieties and frustrations had on the last six chapters of *A Connecticut Yankee*. We must not place too much weight on the writer's personal problems: he had always had trouble ending his books because the reach and power of his imagination tended to outstrip his technical control and even his intellectual grasp of his materials. It is clear on the other hand that the composition of *A Connecticut Yankee* brought into play basic contradictions in Mark Twain's attitudes. In any case, the narrative evidently runs into serious difficulties toward the end. Even though no exact page in the book can be pointed out as marking the moment of collapse, the chapters written during the autumn of 1888 show a growing uncertainty of tone. The style betrays a sense of strain, and there are more and more symptoms of Mark Twain's chronic literary disease, the invasion of his work by clichés and stereotypes borrowed from cheap popular fiction and the melodramatic stage.

The most tangible evidence of breakdown is his loss of the power to make his story carry the symbolic overtones which, despite its unevenness, can be perceived in the first three-quarters of it. The last long sequence that holds up all the way is the adventure of the enchanted pigsty. Brief passages in the Valley of Holiness sequence come off well, such as the Yankee's success in harnessing to a sewing machine the hermit on top of the pillar who bows his body "ceaselessly and rapidly almost to his feet." [31] But there is little in the narrative after the Yankee and the King are sold into slavery which has imaginative solidity. And the device with which Mark Twain broke through the roadblock he had encountered at the end of Chapter XXXVIII, the rescue of the Yankee and the King by a detachment of armored knights on bicycles under the command of Launcelot, has no more literary substance than the arrival of the Fifth Cavalry to the rescue of a wagon train about to be scalped by Indians. The device is particu-

*novel has an
unevenness*

larly unfortunate in that it casts the knights as partisans
of the Yankee and thus blurs the outlines of his campaign to destroy the power of the nobility.

This sacrifice of over-all intention for the sake of a
momentary effect is made the more conspicuous by the
fact that Mark Twain immediately passes on to the
Yankee's duel with Sir Sagramor le Desirous, which
leads to his supposed destruction of knight-errantry.
The reader has difficulty in believing that within the
next three years his revolution is accomplished, except-
ing only the formal proclamation of a republic. Mark
Twain ticks off these portentous changes in a couple
of paragraphs and then veers again toward burlesque
in a speech, attributed to Clarence, about the desirabil-
ity of substituting a family of cats for the royal family.
There is even a digression about baseball teams composed of knights, kings, and emperors. He is improvis-
ing while he gets ready for the finale.

The role of the Yankee is now badly confused. It
will be recalled that he is involved in three conflicts
with three adversaries, each conflict representing a different historical interpretation of the transition from
feudalism to the civilization of the nineteenth century.
The adversaries are the Knights of the Round Table,
defenders of the throne; Merlin; and the Established
Church. Basically, of course, each represents an ob-
stacle in the way of progress, and it is not difficult to
accept in the abstract the notion that Merlin and the
Church join the knights in supporting the monarchic

62

id. with monarchic system

system because their power derives from it. But defining the relation of the several conflicts to one another in terms of plot is another matter. Mark Twain has shown Merlin attempting to aid Sir Sagramor, and he has depicted the theatrical rivalry of the two magicians. Yet he has not found a way to pit the Yankee against the Church in concrete incidents, or to establish the relation between the Church on the one hand and Merlin and the knights on the other. His problem is to contrive a resolution of the plot that will correspond to the necessities of theme.

From an early stage in his work on the book, as we have noticed, Mark Twain had intended to bring the Yankee into head-on collision with the Church by means of an interdict. His notebooks show he had read up for this purpose in historical sources. But he also intended to follow Malory in describing "the disruption of the Round Table" and "that last battle—the Battle of the Broken Hearts." The problem of plotting could be solved, given pains and ingenuity, but only by the invention of a complex series of events that he no longer had the desire or patience to render in detail. Although in a merely technical sense the catastrophe is worked out more plausibly than several earlier sequences, he in effect changes narrators in order to avoid having to describe the collapse of the revolution from the Yankee's own point of view.

In a hurried page or two Mark Twain announces that the Yankee had married Sandy just before the duel

Important — stylistically unevenness shows he is struggling with problemat conce

with Sir Sagramor and that she had borne him a daughter. The child now falls seriously ill with the croup and the parents are advised by the doctors to take her to France for convalescence. This creaky contrivance removes the Yankee from the scene of action so that the actual recital of the crowded events leading to the catastrophe can be entrusted to Clarence. His report, delivered to the Boss on his return to England, resembles the speeches used by popular dramatists to untangle plots and subplots at the end of a conventional melodrama. Clarence punctuates his narrative with such phrases as "End of the first act. Act second, scene first, an apartment in Carlisle castle," and even indicates "*Tableau*" at the end of the scene.[32]

In this fashion the reader learns that Launcelot has bankrupted Sir Mordred and many other knights in a manipulation of railway shares à la Jay Gould. The resentments thus engendered have led to the civil war described by Malory; the mutual self-destruction of the knights is reported in an actual quotation from Malory presented as a bit of war correspondence written by Clarence for his newspaper, the *Weekly Hosannah and Literary Volcano*. The confused factional fighting provided the opportunity the Church had been waiting for and it has issued an interdict directed rather eclectically against both Sir Mordred and the Yankee. When the Church imposes the interdict, even the Man-factories in which the Yankee is training his staff of experts "empty themselves and go over to the

enemy." Speaking through Clarence, Mark Twain ad-
dresses a searching query to the part of himself that had
shared the Yankee's revolutionary hopes:

> "Did you think you had educated the superstition out
> of those people?"
> "I certainly did think it."
> "Well, then, you may unthink it. They stood every
> strain easily—until the Interdict . . . Make up your
> mind to it—when the armies come, the mask will fall." [33]

What follows is one of the most distressing passages
in American literature. The Yankee takes refuge with
Clarence and a small band of loyal boy-technicians in
a cave that Clarence has fortified with Gatling guns,
land mines, and a fence charged with a lethal electric
current. Thirty thousand knights march against them,
and when the anachronistic modern weapons have
done their work, twenty-five thousand corpses lie before the entrance to the cave. The Yankee, placed
under a spell by Merlin in the disguise of an old serving
woman, sleeps thirteen centuries to awaken in Mark
Twain's day and, dying, hand to him the manuscript of
his "Tale of the Lost Land."

The Yankee's disillusionment is remarkably bitter.
When he learns that the Interdict has, as he says, shriv-
eled the common people of Britain into sheep, he ex-
claims: "Imagine such human muck as this; conceive of
this folly!" [34] The crusade against tyranny, the great
project for conferring enlightenment, freedom, and

comfort on the nation by means of an industrial revolution, has ended in failure and despair. Mark Twain's charming dream of himself in armor has revealed deeper and deeper levels of meaning. It has exfoliated into a long book: and has become at the end a nightmare.

See P. Messeda essay —
trace themes — here on in
his later works —
Remember :— Tw's quote tnal
in writing Yankee, he had
unleased personal demons . . . .

3. THE IDEAS IN A DREAM

I

The diverse strains of thought and feeling that converge in the character of Mark Twain's Yankee are all aspects of American self-consciousness in the later nineteenth century, but we can distinguish two clusters of images embodied in this protagonist that derive from radically different sources and are never fully synthesized. In some of his roles the Yankee is a figure out of the past. He is an avatar of the American Adam dwelling in the Garden of the World, whose vague but resplendent features can be discerned in Cooper's Natty Bumppo, the yeoman farmer dear to agrarian tradition, Frederick Jackson Turner's frontiersman, and the idealized "self" of Whitman's *Leaves of Grass*.[1] Because the Yankee is a transatlantic innocent confronting an ancient and corrupt Europe, he also resembles the narrator of *The Innocents Abroad*. In fact, he belongs to the long line of vernacular protagonists in Mark Twain's books which includes the tenderfoot in

Roughing It, the cub pilot in *Life on the Mississippi* and, of course, Huck Finn. The Yankee's colloquial language, his lowly rural origins, his uncultivated practical common sense, and his magnificent indifference toward the pretensions of titled aristocrats all attest to this side of his ancestry. Yet he also embodies significant traits that are foreign to Mark Twain's earlier vernacular characters. One of these novelties is his command of industrial technology. Another is his highly developed political awareness. He is a constitutional and legal theorist and is well versed in the outstanding events of modern history. He knows what he is trying to do in a way that sets him apart from his predecessors.

Although the Yankee is a philistine with reference to the arts, his consciousness of his historical mission makes him an intellectual. Unlike Huck Finn, who is not at ease with concepts, the Yankee is passionately devoted to general ideas such as progress, civilization, justice, equality before the law, universal suffrage, representative government, free trade, and separation of church and state. His principles are American in the sense that they were cherished by virtually all Americans in the nineteenth century, but they are too abstract for folklore and too serious to be useful in comedy, oral or otherwise. In characterizing Hank Morgan, Mark Twain attempted to engraft upon an almost entirely nonintellectual tradition of folk humor an ideology of enlightenment and republicanism.

In the broadest sense, we may say that Mark Twain was trying to depict a protagonist who represented the American common man functioning within an exemplary industrial and political order which he himself created. To put the matter in yet more general terms, Mark Twain was asking himself whether the American Adam, who began as representative of a preindustrial order, could make the transition to urban industrialism and enter upon a new phase of his existence by becoming a capitalist hero. Many of the confusions in the character and actions of Hank Morgan—particularly the extent to which he both is and is not an entrepreneur and businessman—take on clarity and meaning if we examine them in the light of this over-all intention. I shall therefore examine first the vernacular elements in Mark Twain's Yankee and then the functions dictated by his ideology.

II

The vernacular humor of Hank Morgan is his most obvious trait. The device of burlesquing Malory creates almost endless comic opportunities in the handling of romantic conventions of chivalry as if they governed everyday life in Arthurian Britain. To the newcomer from the nineteenth century the inhabitants naturally seem at first simply lunatics. Later he thinks of them as "big boobies" or "white Indians" or tame animals. He analogizes their yarns about forests and enchantments drear with tall tales of the American West, ridicules Malory's endless paratactic sentences as a medium of conversation, takes a common-sense reductionist view of the Grail quest, and notes the impropriety of having high-born damsels accompany knights-errant on long overland journeys without a chaperon. At its best, the burlesque is so brilliant that it disarms criticism, as in the excursion to the enchanted pigsty.

As the story develops, however, the burlesque leads into a bitter vein of satire growing out of the fact that the narrator is an American in conflict with Englishmen. Mark Twain becomes preoccupied with American resentments against nineteenth-century Britain. The years during which he was working on *A Connecticut Yankee* were a period when his patriotism (or rather, his jingoistic nationalism) reached a peak of intensity.[2] The book and its protagonist were thus markedly influenced by an outraged national pride. This emotion was not peculiar to Mark Twain; it was shared by spokesmen for the rising Populist movement and by many other writers and intellectuals, including Howells and Warner, both of whom had defended American ideals and institutions during the 1880's against British criticism. The mood was so pronounced that a debate on the question, "Do Americans hate England?" developed in the magazines toward the end of the decade, culminating in a symposium in the *North American Review* in June 1890. Mark Twain, like many of his countrymen, was particularly annoyed by Matthew

Arnold, who lectured in the United States in 1883–84, and both before and after his visit published a good deal of well-meant advice to the Americans about what needed amendment in their habits and institutions.[3] Mark Twain undoubtedly failed to get Arnold's point, but it must be admitted that the Englishman's lofty tone and his lack of humor might well have irritated a more even-tempered American than Samuel L. Clemens. Arnold concluded that the shortcomings of civilization in the United States could be summed up under the lack of "distinction." To illustrate the vulgarity of American life he cited two phenomena with which Mark Twain was closely identified: the newspapers and the "addiction to 'the funny man,' who is a national misfortune there." [4] Mark Twain's attitude toward the British had wavered over the years; there had been a period when he might even have been described as mildly Anglophile.[5] Now, however, in the 1880's, he reacted violently against what he regarded as British upper-class snobbery, and was led into a correspondingly violent defense of American popular culture. When Andrew Lang, who had put himself on record as an admirer of *Huckleberry Finn*, refused to read *A Connecticut Yankee* because he feared he would be offended by its attacks on British institutions, Mark Twain wrote Lang a letter that is the nearest thing to an apologia he ever composed. In the heat of passion he greatly exaggerated his commitment to American popular culture; within a few years he would veer in the

71

opposite direction to a condemnation of his country-men in such a work as *The American Claimant*. But the letter to Lang nevertheless throws light on the state of mind in which Mark Twain wrote Hank Morgan's diatribes against the injustice and cruelty of British monarchic and aristocratic society. The letter has often been quoted; I shall recall here only a few key phrases. "The thin top crust of humanity," Mark Twain says, is no doubt worthy of attention from elegant writers and critics; but he himself has never been concerned with "the cultivated classes." Instead, he has striven to amuse and edify "the mighty mass of the uncultivated who are underneath." He even asserts belligerently: "I have always catered for the Belly and the Members . . ." [6]

This is the rationale of Hank Morgan's declaration that, being a Yankee of the Yankees, he is practical and nearly devoid of sentiment and poetry. The lack of cultivation familiar in earlier vernacular characters such as Huck Finn takes on here a doctrinaire significance: it has become a positive virtue because at the height of his Anglophobia Mark Twain is disposed to classify refinement and cultivation as snobbish and aristocratic, and to regard philistinism as a necessary concomitant of democracy—and thus of Americanism.

Hank Morgan as quintessential American philistine and democrat has behind him the weight of all Mark Twain's animus against genteel attitudes. The Yankee invader of Arthur's kingdom is "low" in tone. (Dan

72

Beard, the illustrator of the book, appropriately shows him dressed in a loud checked suit and plug hat, swaggering with his hands in his pockets, putting his feet on the furniture, and in one of the most memorable drawings tickling the nose of a gigantic British lion with a straw.) Like the narrator of *The Innocents Abroad*, the Yankee is irreverent because he mocks at the shadowy grandeurs and romantic associations of the age of chivalry in a period when Tennyson's *Idyls of the King* and "Galahad," Lowell's *The Vision of Sir Launfal*, and the paintings of Burne-Jones had canonized feudal knighthood as one of the major symbols of genteel values.

It is significant that on both sides of the Atlantic, the figure of the knight was accepted as the antithesis of the sordid businessman. A reviewer of *A Connecticut Yankee* for the Edinburgh *Scots Observer* called the book "a 'lecture' in dispraise of monarchical institutions and religious establishments as the roots of all evil, and in praise of Yankee 'cuteness and Wall Street chicanery as compared to the simple fidelity . . . of the knightly ideal." [7] The London *Daily Telegraph* stated the question posed by the book as follows: "Which, then, is to be most admired—the supremacy of a knight or the success of a financier? Under which king will the Americans serve—the ideal or the real? Will they owe allegiance to King Arthur or Jay Gould?" [8] In this country, Sidney Lanier's long poem "The Symphony" opposed chivalry to all-blighting trade in a fashion that merges chivalry with Christianity and makes trade the root of all evil.

It will thus be evident that the burlesque of Malory engaged cultural issues of great intensity. As adversary of the Knights of the Round Table the Yankee expresses the irreverence that distressed Mrs. Fairbanks. His aggressive philistinism tends to identify him with the anti-poetic, anti-sentimental businessman. And all these traits cohere about a tendentious image of the democratic American patriot conceived as the antithesis of the typical British aristocrat. Beard was amply justified in making Hank Morgan explicitly into Uncle Sam. In the final sequence the Yankee is suddenly supplied with a suggestive goatee and striped trousers,[9] and he becomes at last fully allegorical with the addition of a top hat bearing a plume labeled "Macaroni." In this drawing the Yankee bestrides a book labeled "Common Sense" and levels a quill pen like a lance at the midriff of a bloated aristocrat suggesting Henry VIII.[10]

But Mark Twain was not prepared at the outset to accept the full implications of the Anglophobia he had invoked in the creation of his protagonist. It will be recalled that in the early chapters he pays rather incongruous tribute to the dignity and grandeur of Launcelot and Galahad; and even after the Yankee has begun his attack on feudalism we are given occasional glimpses of noble behavior such as King Arthur's unhesitating exposure of himself to smallpox when he

bears in his arms a dying child.[11] By and large, however, the vestiges of reverence for the chivalric ideal
are obliterated by the Yankee's increasingly violent
polemic against the feudal order. In comic terms this
takes the form of a campaign to make chivalry ridicu-
lous. The Yankee employs knights as traveling salesmen for stove polish and mouth wash, or as conductors
on railway trains. They are mounted on bicycles; they
play baseball in armor; they are frightened by the pipe
smoke issuing from the visor of his helmet, as if he were
a fire-breathing dragon. The comic contrast between
medieval and modern manners rests on the assumption
that American common sense and commercial realism
are axiomatically superior to the other-worldly inepti-
tude of the knights. The businessman is the moral norm
invoked by the satire: his unromantic usefulness throws
into relief the impractical absurdity of feudalism. This
is the general mood of Mark Twain's readings before
the Military Service Institute in 1886, and the newspaper accounts make clear that not only the audience
of officers, businessmen, and politicians but also the re-
porters were enchanted by the implied endorsement of
American Gilded Age culture and the businessman
ideal.

The mockery of feudalism could of course readily
move beyond vernacular comedy to overt hostility.
We recall that, especially toward the end of the book,
the knights become simply the enemy, to be blown up
by dynamite bombs or shot with revolvers or, at the

he isn't just a mechanic as
he is a owner as well,
a business man.

MARK TWAIN'S

very last, destroyed in a mass slaughter. These expressions of aggressive feeling in the plot are supported by frequent denunciations of the harsh laws and the caste system of Arthur's kingdom. The book amply justifies Mark Twain's description of it to his English publisher as "a Yankee mechanic's say against monarchy and its several natural props." [12] But the values embodied in the character of the Yankee are too largely taken for granted, and the "say against monarchy" replaces the imaginative mode of comedy with mere rhetoric.

III

A Connecticut Yankee could be taken as the expression of an international crusade for democracy. This was the view, for example, of the English publicist W. T. Stead, who praised the book in his newly founded *Review of Reviews*.[13] But American critics tended to identify Hank Morgan's attack on monarchy and aristocracy with his function as avenger of British insults to the United States. A reviewer for the Quincy (California) *Plumas National* rejoiced to find in the book "one long satire on modern England and Englishmen." [14] Dan Beard said he would like to see a copy of *A Connecticut Yankee* in every household in this country because it would help to bring Americans back to "the safe honest and manly position" outlined for them in the Declaration of Independence.[15] Sylvester Baxter, a writer for the Boston *Herald* who was a

end in an
apocalypse

supporter of Edward Bellamy's Nationalism, declared in his laudatory review that "the pages are eloquent with a true American love of freedom . . ." [16]

Like other American readers, Baxter fails to distinguish between two rather different conceptions of the problem of democracy in the modern world. Sometimes he seems to regard the democratic cause as an American monopoly, identifying it with hostility to a Britain that serves as an anti-democratic symbol. At other times he praises Mark Twain for an attitude that does not seem to be related to national boundaries—a general "sympathy with the rights of the common people, and an indignant hatred of oppression of the poor, the lowly and the weak, by the rich, the powerful and the proud." Howells' long and interesting essay on *A Connecticut Yankee* [17] emphasizes this broadly humanitarian reading of the book, yet he sometimes attributes contemporary abuses primarily to Britain. He takes the book to be something like *Uncle Tom's Cabin* —an indictment of oppressive institutions by means of incidents revealing the injustices visited on helpless and innocent victims, with Hank Morgan playing such a role as John Brown might have played in Mrs. Stowe's slaveholding South. The descriptions of commoners caged in dungeons, tortured on the rack, starved, beaten, shackled in slavery, or hanged for trivial offenses, he says, ". . . wring the heart for what has been of cruelty and wrong in the past . . ." Howells' theoretical devotion to realism in fiction is evidently overwhelmed by his sympathy for the downtrodden masses. By calling the book a romance he can welcome it as an allegorical depiction of injustices in the modern world. The story, he says, leaves the reader "burning with shame and hate for the conditions which are of like effect in the present. It is one of its magical properties that the fantastic fable of Arthur's far-off time is also too often the sad truth of ours . . ." Concerning the "heartbreaking scene" of the young mother hanged for theft to keep her child from starving, he writes:

> It is one of the many passages in the story where our civilization of to-day sees itself mirrored in the cruel barbarism of the past, the same in principle, and only softened in custom. With shocks of consciousness, one recognizes in such episodes that the laws are still made for the few against the many, and that the preservation of things, not men, is still the ideal of legislation.

"Our civilization" seems to include the United States. Yet when he grows more specific he might be interpreted as referring to England alone:

> The elastic scheme of the romance allows it to play freely back and forward between the sixth century and the nineteenth . . . ; and often while it is working the reader up to a blasting contempt of monarchy and aristocracy in King Arthur's time, the dates are magically shifted under him, and he is confronted with exactly the same principles in Queen Victoria's time.

78

The first critic—after his wife—to whom Mark Twain submitted the manuscript of the completed work was the stockbroker-poet, Edmund C. Stedman, who was editing an eleven-volume *Library of American Literature* for Clemens' publishing house. On 7 July 1889 Stedman returned the manuscript with warm praise. He asserted: "You are going at the *still existing* radical principles or fallacies which made 'chivalry' possible once, & servilities & flunkeyism & tyranny possible now." [18] The supposed bearing of the book on contemporary society is emphasized and extended in Beard's illustrations, which, as some reviewers noticed, constituted a drastic reading-in of radical doctrines only faintly suggested, or not suggested at all, in Mark Twain's text. Most of Beard's drawings are deft, witty commentaries on the story, but far too many of them are crude cartoons that make their point only by means of elaborate labels. In this fashion Beard ascribes to Mark Twain a number of slogans and battle cries of current left-wing groups such as the Single-Taxers and the Anti-Monopolists with whom he had had no previous association. One of Beard's more extreme flights of fancy shows two allegorical female figures representing Justice in the sixth and nineteenth centuries, each peeking out from behind the bandage covering her eyes, and each holding a balance in which a hammer marked "Labor" is outweighed—in the sixth century by a crown or coronet labeled "Title," in the nineteenth century by a moneybag labeled "$1000000." [19]

There are numerous other illustrations of this sort, the total effect of which was well described by an anonymous critic in Henry George's New York *Standard*:

> Though but little is said in the book about specific social or political reforms, it is impossible to read these extracts [quoted in the review] without seeing that the great American humorist has been moved by the spirit of democracy. Human equality, natural rights, unjust laws, class snobbery, the power of the rich and the dependence and oppression of the poor, are subjects of frequent allusion in the text; and whatever of definiteness the text may lack in pointing out the fundamental cause and radical cure for wrongs, is admirably supplied by Dan Beard in the illustrations.[20]

A particularly dubious inference from the story—almost certainly misrepresenting the views of Mark Twain, who was never disposed to question private rights in property—is set forth in one of the illustrations reproduced by the *Standard*. Over the caption "The Coming Eclipse," the drawing shows a sun labeled "Divine Right of Kings VI Cen" about to be obscured by a sphere labeled "The Earth Belongs to the People XIX Cen," while a huddled throng kneel or lift up their hands in salutation.[21] The passage near which the drawing is placed does contain a denunciation of the divine right of kings by the Yankee, but there is nothing in the text to support Beard's single-tax doctrine about ownership of natural resources.

A more defensible use of illustrations to go beyond the letter of the text is Beard's amusing depiction of living Englishmen in the guise of unsympathetic characters in the story. He gives to Merlin the venerable features of Tennyson, and to a "chuckleheaded" nobleman the countenance of the Prince of Wales.[22] But the distinction between legitimate and illegitimate interpretation of the book in Beard's drawings was of no moment to Mark Twain, who complicated the task of future critics by unqualified praise of the illustrations as a whole.[23] One can only conclude that by the time he had finished the book he was perfectly willing to accept the opinions of his associates about its meaning. Howells also asserted that Beard had accurately captured the spirit of the text. In the general humanitarian and Populist enthusiasm, fine shades of doctrine were of little interest to either the writer or his readers.

Simply as a literary idea, the notion of viewing the European past through the eyes of an adult spokesman for the American vernacular tradition was as promising as any Mark Twain had ever hit upon. It was a misfortune that he allowed himself to be diverted from his original plan into the well-worn ruts of Anglophobia and sentimental melodrama. Both the attack on nineteenth-century England and the doctrinaire polemic against feudalism were essentially irrelevant to the imaginative core of the story. The crude hostility to which Mark Twain committed himself in this fashion ruled out any approach to the ironic complexity of vision that he had achieved in *Huckleberry Finn*.

IV

The transition from a comic to a melodramatic mode evident in the passages that wrung Howells' heart indicates that Mark Twain had begun to draw upon a store of ideas and attitudes quite different from the motives he had taken over from native backwoods humor. He had implied as much when he told Mrs. Fairbanks he was writing a contrast of civilizations. The contrast, of course, was between poverty-stricken, ignorant, tyrannical feudalism and the enlightened industrial capitalism of the nineteenth century. Mark Twain, in common with virtually all his contemporaries, held to a theory of history that placed these two civilizations along a dimension stretching from a backward abyss of barbarism toward a Utopian future of happiness and justice for all mankind. The code name for the historical process thus displayed was progress, and in nineteenth-century America it had the status of a secular theology.[24]

The current notion of progress had a considerable basis in Mark Twain's own experience. For he had himself passed from the tranquil preindustrial world of Hannibal in the 1840's to Hartford in the highly industrialized Connecticut Valley, where during most of the 1880's he had been preoccupied with what he considered the most amazing of modern inventions, the Paige typesetter. The sixth-century Britain of Hank Morgan's adventures shows many points of similarity to the slaveholding Missouri of Mark Twain's childhood. The prewar South, for example, is described in *Life on the Mississippi* as having been debilitated by a chivalry-disease contracted from reading Walter Scott's medieval romances,[25] and in *Pudd'nhead Wilson* Mark Twain would implant a hollow but fanatically cherished ideal of chivalry in Dawson's Landing, one of his many versions of Hannibal.[26] The institution of slavery introduced unhistorically into Arthurian Britain is documented with incidents drawn from the supposedly authentic *Autobiography* of Charles Ball, an American Negro slave. Hank Morgan explicitly compares the peasants of Abblasoure Manor with the misguided poor whites who served in the ranks of the Confederate Army to defend an aristocratic order that kept them degraded and impoverished.[27] Most significant of all, perhaps, the landscape of Britain is described by means of words and images identical with those Mark Twain would apply in his *Autobiography* to the Quarles Farm near Hannibal that he had known as a boy.[28]

Thus Mark Twain's own observation had deeply impressed upon him the pattern of rapid transition from a backward agrarian society with corrupt institutions and ideals to an industrial society enjoying all the benefits of machine technology and enlightened republican government. The contrast between medieval and modern civilizations was, accordingly, the obvious conceptual framework for the Yankee's adventures in Arthurian Britain.

The most obvious exemplification of progress in the story is the Yankee's technological achievements—his creation of a complex of factories, railways, and telegraph and telephone lines. This aspect of the contrast between civilizations is an allegory of the industrial revolution; its emphasis is primarily economic. But the contrast also has a political aspect in the depiction of outrageous laws by means of which the nobles of Arthur's realm oppress the people. In this respect the story is an allegory of the French Revolution, which the Yankee mentions with enthusiasm.

Hank Morgan was meant to be a representative American both in his practical knowledge of machines and in his devotion to republican institutions. But at different times Mark Twain emphasized first one aspect and then the other. His introductory remarks for readings from the unfinished manuscript before a Baltimore audience in January 1888 stressed the Yankee's technology:

> Conceive of the blank & sterile ignorance of that day, & contrast it with the vast & many-sided knowledge of this. Consider the trivial miracles & wonders wrought by the humbug magicians & enchanters of that old day, & contrast them with the mighty miracles wrought by science in our day of steam & electricity. Take a practical man, thoroughly equipped with the scientific [magic]

84

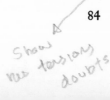

enchantments of our day & set him down alongside of Merlin the head magician of Arthur's time, & what sort of a show would Merlin stand? [29]

Here, evidently, "civilization" is equated with knowledge, and knowledge with technology. Chapter X of the novel, describing the creation of the Yankee's hidden industrial system, is entitled "Beginnings of Civilization." To mention only one other passage, when Clarence reports his preparations for a last stand in Merlin's cave, he explicitly refers to "all our vast factories, mills, workshops, magazines, etc." as "our civilization." [30]

After the book was published Mark Twain continued on various occasions to interpret "civilization" in similar fashion. Thus in an unpublished reply to Paul Bourget's criticism of the United States (probably written in 1894) he sets out to list the components of modern civilization, most of which he claims as American contributions. The first five items are political and legal: "Political Liberty," "Religious Liberty," "Reduction of Capital Penalties," "Man's Equality before the Law," and "Woman's rights." But No. 6 is "Application of Anaesthesia in Surgery." And with No. 7 ("The First Approximately Rational Patent Law") and No. 8 ("Development of Patents") he begins a list of mechanical inventions that reaches almost one hundred items before the writer begins to tire of the game.[31]

Despite Mark Twain's stated beliefs, however, the

theme of technological advance is only meagerly dealt with in *A Connecticut Yankee*. Man-factories are mentioned, but the only products of the Yankee's system of technical education that appear on stage are the fifty-two shadowy boy technicians in the cave at the end, none of them given an identity or even a name, and none represented as performing any concrete action. Despite Mark Twain's occasional efforts to give fictional substance to the Yankee's mechanical prowess, he actually performs no constructive feat except the restoration of the holy well; and it will be recalled that the technology in this episode does not go into repairing the well, but into the fraudulent display of fireworks with which he awes the populace.

One of the reasons why the Yankee provides so little actual demonstration of his technological skill is his curious passivity during most of the narrative. After emphasizing at the outset the protagonist's ability to build or invent all kinds of machinery, Mark Twain seems strangely reluctant to make use of this power in the story. By far the longest and most vivid sequences are those in which the Yankee is not a mover and shaker but a spectator or victim of feudal oppression. The narrative viewpoint in these chapters resembles that in the middle section of *Huckleberry Finn*, where the Duke and the King dominate Huck by the threat of turning Jim in as a runaway slave. Huck is powerless to resist and can merely record the brutality and degradation he witnesses in the towns along the shore of the

86

Mississippi. Through almost five hundred pages of *A Connecticut Yankee* Hank Morgan is restrained for one reason or another from full exercise of the powers theoretically conferred on him at the outset when he is made "perpetual minister and executive" to the King, "the second personage in the Kingdom, as far as political power and authority were concerned." During his first seven years in office he postpones overt action because he must build his factories and workshops before he can openly defy the Church and the nobles. He is constrained by opinion at the court to set out on his travels with Sandy, during which he ceases to function as an executive. The device of sending the Yankee traveling about the kingdom in disguise with the King is yet another way of depriving him temporarily of administrative responsibility; and having him sold into slavery renders him completely helpless. Thus through the greater part of the book the Yankee is unable to enact the role of entrepreneur that Mark Twain putatively assigns to him. His program for industrializing Britain appears only in such trivial items as the knights made to serve as traveling salesmen or the bicycles on which Launcelot and the Knights ride from Camelot to London.

Furthermore, even when the stage is set for exhibitions of modern technology, the effect falls short of expectation. Again and again—in the Yankee's exploitation of the eclipse, in the destruction of Merlin's tower, in the restoration of the well—a minimum of science or technology is overlaid by elaborate and essentially fraudulent display. Hank Morgan is at least half as much a pretender as Merlin is; the spectacle surrounding his miracles has hardly more empirical basis than do Merlin's charms and spells, the "fol-de-rol" of which he is so scornful. The reader eventually begins to wonder whether Mark Twain may not have been unduly influenced by the current habit of speaking about science and technology as mysterious and magical. When the Yankee refers to his "miracles," he is perhaps only half joking. His statement to Merlin, "I am going to call down fire and blow up your tower," [32] claims a quasi-mythical status that Mark Twain seems inclined to grant him; for the spark that ignites the charges of gunpowder is provided through lightning rods by a thunderstorm at precisely the moment chosen by the Yankee for his theatrical demonstration.

To regard the engineer's work as supernatural is of course to view it with the awe of an outsider, an uncomprehending layman. The fact is that despite Clemens' interest in gadgets and machines—particularly the Paige typesetter—he did not really understand what the experts were doing; indeed, no one without technical training could have understood it. The technological feats that Mark Twain ascribes to his protagonist had not entered deeply enough into his experience to be fully grasped by his imagination. Wordsworth had predicted that the poet would "be ready to follow the steps of the Man of Science . . . carrying sensa-

tion into the midst of the objects of the science itself,"
but only when "these things shall be familiar to us,
. . . manifestly and palpably material to us as enjoying
and suffering beings." [33] Melville had learned whaling
by shipping before the mast, and he could therefore
work this relatively primitive technology into the fab-
ric of his fiction. But no American writer in the 1880's
knew enough about even the simplest power-driven
machines to subdue them to the uses of literature. For
that matter, has anyone yet been able to write the fictional interpretation of modern technology that Mark
Twain tried to produce?

Magic, of course, can be black as well as white; and
along with the implication that the Yankee's machines
will work miracles for the good of mankind, the reader
notices strong hints that they are potentially a menace.
Since this evidence has been discussed by several critics,
all that need be said here is that the twenty-five thousand rotting corpses left before the cave when the elec-
trically charged fences and Gatling guns have done
their work are but the culmination of a series of half-
buried suggestions all through the narrative. In an often
quoted passage in Chapter X, for example, the Yankee
compares his hidden factories to a "serene volcano,
standing innocent with its smokeless summit in the blue
sky and giving no sign of the rising hell in its bow-
els." [34]

[handwritten margin notes: see p 97-8 / "unlimited" way / Isn't Tech appears / significant things: / weapons / destruction / fraud/vaudeville / vague/threatening "undesigned" / factories]

V

The inadequate development of the theme of technology seriously impairs the contrast of civilizations in the story. Mark Twain devotes much more attention to material that is in a broad sense political—the various procedures for demonstrating the evils of feudalism and the merits of republican government. Yet here also he runs into difficulties. The polemic against feudalism implies an unqualified endorsement of the American system of government, which the Yankee makes explicit by comments such as his quotation of the Constitution of Connecticut to the effect that "all political power is inherent in the people." [35] In the abstract, his program rests on the assumption that under free political institutions, industrialization will achieve Utopian results without interference by the state: the classical doctrine of laissez-faire liberalism. Mr. Louis J. Budd has demonstrated that, generally speaking, Mark Twain shared the belief in this doctrine held in his day by all but the most extreme left-wing thinkers.[36]

Yet there are a number of indications in *A Connecticut Yankee* that he was troubled by growing doubts concerning the liberal creed. Like Warner and Howells, he had misgivings about the unrestrained operation of the profit motive. His uneasiness appears in his ambiguous handling of the Yankee's commercial ambitions. The early chapters present the protagonist as a cunning operator bent on making money. When Hank Morgan says that if an eclipse of the moon had been imminent he could have sold it short, or that "Merlin's stock was flat," the most obvious effect is of comic incongruity between this jargon of the stock market and the tone of Malory's fictive world. Nevertheless, the cumulative effect of the Yankee's commercial imagery is to suggest detachment on Mark Twain's part. The Yankee's exploitation of the eclipse is of course justifiable as a means of saving his life, but the manner in which he takes advantage of the situation to make himself economic master of the country seems somewhat cynical. The very title "The Boss" in which he takes so much pleasure has unpleasant overtones ("Boss" Tweed of Tammany had been a household word in the United States since the 1860's). Only later, when the Yankee becomes preoccupied with his attack on feudalism and loses interest in economic activity, does Mark Twain identify himself with the narrator. And even then his distaste for merely commercial motives continues to reappear occasionally—as for example in the Yankee's gleeful and self-satisfied account of his debasement of the currency or, more strongly, in the complacency of his remark that when he noticed signs of a breakdown in the hermit harnessed to a sewing machine, "I stocked the business and unloaded, taking Sir Bors de Ganis into camp financially along with certain of his friends: for the works stopped within a year, and the good saint got him to his rest." [37]

On the other hand, in the final sequence, when Launcelot buys up wildcat railway stock and bankrupts Sir Agravaine and Sir Mordred, Clarence comments with the writer's apparent approval: "He skinned them alive, and they deserved it—anyway, the whole kingdom rejoiced." [38] Many of the references to speculation here and elsewhere have a certain innocence, as if Mark Twain were simply amusing himself by applying to the Knights of the Round Table terms borrowed from the stock market. This vein of humor harks back to the irresponsible gaiety of his journalism in the 1860's. The connection with earlier comic devices is particularly close in the Yankee's casual comparison of his own plans with Joseph's "splendid financial ingenuities." Such verbal horseplay may well have had no connection in the writer's mind with the realities of Gilded Age financial piracies. Yet Mark Twain undoubtedly felt some of the distaste for large-scale speculation that was so deep-seated in Warner and Howells. More than one reviewer of *A Connecticut Yankee* noticed that Beard had given the instantly recognizable features of Jay Gould to a slave driver represented in a full-page drawing as standing with a whip in his hand and one foot planted on the breast of a prostrate female slave.[39] Sylvester Baxter referred to the picture and characterized Gould as a notorious billionaire and stock gambler. The satirical allusion had no basis in the text, but when

Mark Twain was interviewed by a reporter for the New York *Times*, he said he was "delighted at the way the artist has entered into the spirit of the book in executing the illustrations, and pointed specially to a fine portrait of Jay Gould in the capacity of 'the slave driver.' " [40]

In later years Mark Twain became convinced that financial tycoons had had an evil influence on American civilization. During the last decade of his life he jotted down a revealing page of notes for an essay on recent American history:

THE START. Benton—Pac. RR—only 3 rich men then, of very humble origin: Astor, skins, Girard (college—stolen) Vand. boating—in Cin (Longworth) . . . not another in Amer. Vand. first to consolidate a trust. Gould followed CIVIL WAR & California sudden-riches disease with a *worse* one, s.r. [secured riches?] by swindling & buying courts. Cal. & Gould were the beginners of the moral rot, they were the worst things that ever befel Amer; they created the hunger for wealth when the Gr. Civ. had just completed its youth & its ennobling WAR—strong, pure, clean, ambitious, impressionable—ready to make choice of a life-course & move with a rush; *they* & *circumstances* determined the choice. . . . Circumst. after Vand. wrought railways into systems; then Standard Oil; Steel Trust; & Carnegie. CALIF—causes Pac. R. R. UNCLE TOM WAR TELEGRAPH. to *restrict* slavery—circum. *abolished* it. GOULD, R. by theft.—R.R. wrecker & buyer of courts. CABLE. CONSOLIDATION invented by Vander.

Other RRs follow. STAND. O. begins CON of *Manu-fac*. FILIPINE & S.A.–CHINA. MORGAN consolidates steel, copper, cables, ships, the WORLD's commerce–Europe began to decline.[41]

At this point the projected essay looks toward a future in which Morgan takes over all power in the United States, "meditates a monarchy," and in short consummates the liquidation of the American republican experiment. For our purposes it is enough to notice that Gould is bracketed with the California gold rush as one of the two "worst things that ever befel America."

Although Mark Twain may not have reached this degree of hostility toward financiers at the time he wrote *A Connecticut Yankee*, the transformation of the Round Table into a stock exchange and the outbreak of civil war in the kingdom as a result of financial rivalries cannot be wholly devoid of meaning. Just as the Yankee's technological revolution tends to dwindle into a rather childish contest with Merlin, so his creation of an industrial system leads to economic anarchy rather than an orderly and prosperous society. Mark Twain's difficulties in plot construction were paralleled by difficulties in developing the themes of his story. Hank Morgan's vernacular common sense and freedom from pretense veered off into Anglophobia. His plan for proclaiming a republic was frustrated by the operations of speculators. These perversions of the thematic pattern bespeak a crisis in Mark Twain's thought and feeling about progress, a crisis so severe that it led to an almost complete loss of control over his materials. The world of the novel falls into a chaos which is reflected in the diction, the tone, the very rhythms of the prose. The contrast of civilizations drops from sight, and the Yankee's Promethean mission ends in absolute failure.

The debacle is foreshadowed here and there throughout the latter half of the novel, but it becomes overwhelmingly evident in the last six chapters. Let us go back somewhat in time within the story to examine this final sequence.

VI

The inevitable showdown between the Yankee and the Knights of the Round Table has been postponed through hundreds of pages while Mark Twain has filled out his indictment of feudal society. It comes at last, however, quite abruptly in Chapter XXXIX with the duel between Hank Morgan and Sir Sagramor le Desirous. The writer tries to draw together here the economic and the political strands of the plot. The Yankee declares that "the life of knight-errantry" is at stake in the duel. As if Mark Twain were trying to lay hold again upon the temporarily forgotten contrast of civilizations, the Yankee recapitulates his original self-characterization by describing himself as "the champion of hard unsentimental common sense and reason" entering the lists "to either destroy knight-errantry or be its victim." Thus "every knight was there who had any ambition or any caste feeling; for my feeling toward their order was not much of a secret, and so here was their chance. If I won my fight with Sir Sagramor, others would have the right to call me out as long as I might be willing to respond." Mark Twain gives the duel further symbolic meaning by enlisting Merlin in Sir Sagramor's cause, with renewed hints of supernatural forces at work: the Yankee declares that Merlin's support of Sir Sagramor makes the forthcoming fight "a duel between two mighty magicians; a duel not of muscle but of mind, not of human skill but of superhuman art and craft; a final struggle for supremacy between the two master enchanters of the age."

Since this encounter is evidently meant to symbolize the Yankee's technological as well as his political triumph, Mark Twain's language is worth careful inspection. The passage flickers with irony; it can be read in several senses. The most obvious meaning is of course that Merlin is only a fraud, with no real power, whereas the Yankee wields the true power of science, which is magical only in the eyes of ignorant spectators. But the Yankee implies that he and Merlin are almost evenly matched. He seems proud to become the adversary of so formidable a magician. And if the Yankee and Merlin stand on an even footing, two other readings are suggested: (1) Both Merlin and the Yankee are frauds. This reading gains plausibility from the fact that the Yankee's magic turns out to consist of a cowboy's lasso and six-shooters. (2) Or the statement can be construed to mean that both Merlin and the Yankee actually do have magical powers, even though the Yankee's may be the stronger. This reading is supported by the Yankee's oratorical tone and by his growing tendency to a kind of megalomania.

Despite this portentous advance billing, however, the actual combat has an anticlimactic air of vaudeville. The Yankee dresses for the fray in the costume of a circus acrobat ("flesh-colored tights from neck to heel, with blue silk puffings about my loins"), and his horse is described with dime-novel seriousness: it is "not above medium size, but . . . alert, slender-limbed, muscled with watch-springs, and just a greyhound to go." Furthermore, his weapons resemble the stage properties of a Wild West show. The effect is so incongruous that we are forced to try to account for it. Perhaps the explanation lies in the mood of jingoistic Americanism that has been building up in Mark Twain. Sir Sagramor, backed by Merlin, is a champion of feudalism and thus a suitable adversary for the Yankee conceived as a representative of modern civilization. But Mark Twain perceives the duel with a double vision. Although Hank Morgan is ostensibly a nineteenth-century hero assailing medieval tyranny and superstition, he is covertly a plebeian Yankee doing battle with the British aristocracy of Victoria's day. In this capacity he must be as American as possible: and what was more spectacularly indigenous than a cow-

97

No:- he is also a coldblooded murderer - using tech. in this way-

boy? Once the idea of turning the tournament into a Buffalo Bill performance was accepted, the circus costume would seem only a slight extension of it—with the additional merit of putting into visual terms Hank Morgan's insatiable exhibitionism.

Whether these conjectures are accurate or not, the slapstick tone of the episode shows that Mark Twain is in some way inhibited from doing justice to his ideological investment in it. He tries to achieve by arbitrary assertion an effect that is not realized in imaginative terms. After the Yankee has killed Sir Sagramor with his revolver, he issues a general challenge: "Here I stand, and dare the chivalry of England to come against me—not by individuals, but in mass!" There is a charge of knights, but when he has killed nine more of them (of course he is a two-gun man), the survivors break and run. The Yankee's comment on this outcome invokes once more the image of the French Revolution: "The day was mine. Knight-errantry was a doomed institution. The march of civilization was begun." And he immediately moves into the final phase of his program: ". . . the very next day I exposed my hidden schools, my mines, and my vast system of clandestine factories and workshops to an astonished world. That is to say, I exposed the nineteenth century to the inspection of the sixth."

The time seems to have come for Mark Twain to show precisely how industrialization remakes men and institutions in a desirable modern pattern. If the contrast between civilizations is to be worked out, we expect a description of capitalist society comparable to the detailed picture of the feudal order that has occupied the bulk of the narrative. But our expectation is disappointed. No more than a few sketchy paragraphs are devoted to the new industrial order before the final catastrophe. The sudden shift in tone, conspicuous even in this uneven novel; the hurried, perfunctory winding-up of the plot; and especially the frightening violence of the final Battle of the Sand Belt, reveal that the original scheme has been abandoned. The Yankee can destroy knight-errantry but he cannot create a viable system to take its place. He seems quite unprepared for the sudden collapse of his program, and in view of the increasing signs of identification between author and protagonist, Mark Twain must have suffered that disillusionment himself.

VII

There is a curious analogy between the Yankee's effort to industrialize Britain and Mark Twain's effort to construct a fictional model of nineteenth-century American capitalism. Like every artist, he was by instinct an idealist in philosophy: things became real for him in proportion as he could give them imaginative substance. Whether consciously or not, in writing *A Connecticut Yankee* he was attempting to justify his belief in the superiority of the American economic and po-

99

litical system by creating a favorable image of it in fiction. This involved presenting in concrete detail a complex of institutions that had previously been little more than a vague abstraction for him. It was a heroic undertaking—one that had not even occurred to Warner and Howells. If he could have brought it off, he would have written a novel on the scale of *War and Peace* or *The Charterhouse of Parma*. His failure is not surprising, and in inquiring into the causes of it we must remember that only a great artist could have made the attempt at all.

Nevertheless, he did fail, and the circumstances throw light on the difficulties that stood in the way of any American writer who tried to take stock of what was happening to his country in the decades after the Civil War. It will help us to realize Mark Twain's predicament if we recall that his contemporary Henry Adams, after decades spent in trying to understand the new forces at work in the late nineteenth century, concluded that they could not be grasped by the human mind because they were outside the domain of consciousness.[42]

Mark Twain faced two principal difficulties in dealing with the new American capitalism, both resulting from the narrative conception with which he began. This scheme implies that the whole of modern civilization is incarnated in the Hartford mechanic who is transported to sixth-century Britain. Under such an arrangement, it is impossible to represent adequately the

100

internal tensions and conflicts that characterize a complex industrial society. For example, since Hank Morgan is both a worker and an employer, there is no way to take account of the clashes between labor and management that were so conspicuous in this country in the 1870's and 1880's. Although the Yankee is the superintendent of what must be imagined as thousands of factory workers, nothing is said in the story about wages, conditions of work, unemployment, strikes, and so on. The industrial system seems to operate with no internal friction; the Yankee's difficulties are caused exclusively by the church and the feudal aristocracy.

Mark Twain was, of course, fully aware of the possibility of violent collisions between employers and workers in industry. The strike at the McCormick plant in Chicago which resulted in the Haymarket Riots was only one of many spectacular industrial conflicts that had filled headlines year after year since the first nationwide railroad strikes in the 1870's. In an essay written in 1886 when he was just beginning his novel, he had declared that industrial workers were on the point of organizing themselves into a vast union resembling the Knights of Labor, and by this means would take over direction of the economy from their enemies, the managers and corporations.[43] But the explanation for his failure to perceive the implications of his own theory can be found in this same paper. He says that the managers and corporations of the modern world are the equivalents of the nobles and kings of the feudal era. Because Hank Morgan is the enemy of the Arthurian nobility, Mark Twain thinks of him as a worker rather than a manager. Mark Twain's rage against the English aristocracy, medieval and modern, was so great that he assumed the Yankee and his workers had a common cause against their enemies, just as he assumed that all Americans had the same grievances against England. The commitment to getting the job done that the Yankee shares with his assistant Clarence and their vaguely depicted subordinates makes them resemble in some respects the corps of technicians and engineers Thorstein Veblen would later endorse as the best rulers of the state. After all, the Yankee was a vernacular hero impatient of ceremonial frills and bent on destroying an idle and barbaric leisure class.

The second odd feature of the Yankee's industrial society is that it seems to have little or no financial system. All fixed capital belongs to the state; the Boss simply does business with himself. He administers the industrial complex for the common good, presumably reinvesting the profits and distributing consumer goods without regard to prices. For all we are told in the story, the sewing machines and typewriters that he mentions are simply issued to the inhabitants of the kingdom instead of being sold. There are to be sure a few touches implying the existence of some kind of currency. The knights who ride about the countryside advertising soap and mouth wash are peddlers of these commodities. But such casual references do not give a clear idea of how the economics of retail sales were managed. The discussion of wages and prices at the dinner table of Marco the charcoal burner leaves the impression that the common people could not possibly have had enough money to buy the articles produced by the Yankee's factories, and nothing is said later about an increase of purchasing power in the populace.

Since finance is of minor consequence in the Yankee's industrialized society, the type of businessman who has made himself a millionaire through speculation—in the manner of Howells' Dryfoos and Warner's Hollowell—cannot exist in it. Mark Twain ignores the type-figure who embodies for Warner and Howells the most glaring evils of the new capitalism. Although Launcelot and his colleagues speculate in railroad stocks, they seem to be engaged in a game—something like Monopoly—rather than a contest for control of actual corporations. Money has no relation to power. Railroad wrecking in the manner of Henderson and Hollowell is impossible because Hank Morgan controls all the industrial enterprises he has fostered. Thus there is no real competition among tycoons, and the economic system lacks another of the most conspicuous traits of the American world of business in the later nineteenth century.

In the absence of rich operators, the Yankee's Britain can offer no instances of the kind of corrupt influence of business on government that Warner makes much of—and that Mark Twain attributed to Gould and

Morgan in his later notes. By virtue of the Yankee's position as The Boss, he merges in himself the functions of ownership, management, and government. The title to the new factories is vested in the state, and he may be imagined as issuing his directives in the name of the King, but in effect he is an economic dictator, or in his own terms a "despot." [44] From the standpoint of economics, the society he brings into being resembles Soviet Russia rather than nineteenth-century America, or any free-enterprise system.

VIII

Mark Twain could not work out adequately his contrast of medieval and modern civilizations because the protagonist who represented the modern world in the story was an inadequate vehicle for depicting industrial capitalism. In more metaphorical terms, the American Adam representing an older agrarian or pre-agrarian order could not be made into a Prometheus creating and administering an economic system comparable in complexity to the actual economic system of post-Civil War America.

Adam and Prometheus—American Adam and American Prometheus—are cultural symbols, and to state Mark Twain's dilemma in these terms is to imply that the failure of his undertaking in *A Connecticut Yankee* was due to forces affecting all perceptive men of his generation—including for example Henry Adams, who found that the modern world resisted his effort to interpret it by means of scientific concepts, and Frederick Jackson Turner, whose archetypal frontiersman was even less able than Hank Morgan to function in an urban industrial society because he knew nothing about machine technology.[45] Warner and Howells, of course, were condemned to failure from the beginning because they had no categories of interpretation except a set of outmoded moral principles.

Yet if Hank Morgan's story can be read as a parable dealing with the same historical subject as *The Education of Henry Adams*, his defeat is also due to a conflict within Mark Twain's mind between a conscious endorsement of progress and a latent revulsion against the non-human imperatives of the machine and all it stood for in the way of discipline and organization.[46] Again, Mark Twain was not alone in experiencing such emotions; much evidence has been gathered to demonstrate the existence of a "covert culture" in this country from the early nineteenth century onwards which associated machines with images of destruction and menace.[47] But his latent hostility to machines and technological progress was unusually strong. Even though he disclaimed exact fidelity to history, his choice of medieval Britain as the setting for his fable meant that he could not hope to represent the Yankee's undertaking as permanently successful. Mark Twain may not have realized fully at the outset what the implications of this decision were, but they must have been present in his mind in some

105

fashion. Let me mention again the evidences in the story itself that he felt a nostalgia for a half-remembered, half-imagined preindustrial world: the images associated with his uncle's farm near Hannibal that crop up so vividly in his descriptions of landscapes in Arthurian Britain; the hints that the Yankee's industrial system is a potential menace; the consistently destructive effects of technology in the story; and above all the strange ending of the framework narrative, in which the dying Yankee proclaims himself to be "a stranger and forlorn" in the modern world, "with an abyss of thirteen centuries yawning . . . between me and all that is dear to me, all that could make life worth the living!" [48]

These words are addressed in delirium to his beloved Sandy; his yearning for his Lost World is expressed in conventional terms, but it is nevertheless erotic. Since the Lost World is also identified with memories of childhood, one might conjecture that Mark Twain's latent hostility to industrialism is related to the psychological conflict between Eros and civilization that Herbert Marcuse has explored. [49] But the prelogical fantasies of this sort are buried too deeply to be more than glimpsed. The overt narrative presents a conflict expressed in terms more congruous with Hank Morgan's announced effort to bring enlightenment and progress to medieval Britain. He identifies the force that has defeated him as "superstition," the structure of habit imposed on all men by the conditions of their lives in society.[50] Another name for this ineradicable evil is "training," the conditioning that implants reverence for established authority in every man's mind from childhood.[51] The brute fact is that men love their chains and turn against the saviors who would force freedom on them. In the final sequence of the novel, the human fear of rationality seems categorical and primal: it is a secularized version of Original Sin, and no means of redemption is in sight.

Mark Twain's proclamation of this doctrine through a protagonist with whom he is now fully identified reveals an absolute despair. It is true that his comments on the book after it was finished show he was not fully conscious of its meaning. Nevertheless, at some point in the composition of this fable he had passed the great divide in his career as a writer. What had happened to him was too complex to be made out at this distance in time, but one aspect of it is clear. When he found it impossible to show how the values represented by his vernacular protagonist could survive in an industrial society, he lost his faith in the value system of that society. Henceforth he worked as a writer in a kind of spiritual vacuum. His imagination was virtually paralyzed. He was never again able to reach the level of his achievement in *Adventures of Huckleberry Finn*. Frustrated in his attempt to come to terms with the industrial revolution, he gave up the modern world for lost, and during the rest of his career devoted most of his energy to composing variations on the theme expressed in his slogan of "the damned human race." That indomitable writer's imagination of his spent itself for two decades in a series of demonstrations that, as the dying Yankee believed, the world is too absurd to be anything but a dream.[52]

A Yankee stands in the chronology of Twain's work as 'the shape of things to come'

NOTES

Chapter I

1. "A Bibliographical Survey of Economic and Political Writings, 1865–1900," *American Literature*, XV (January, 1944), 409.
2. *Dictionary of American English*, s.v. "capitalism"; Augustus A. Levy, "The Newspaper Habit and its Effects," *North American Review*, CXLIII (September, 1886), 312.
3. Albion W. Tourgée, *Murvale Eastman, Christian Socialist* (New York, 1890), pp. i–iii.
4. Andrew Carnegie, "Wealth," *North American Review*, CXLVIII (June, 1889), 655.
5. "The Gilded Age" (1873), in *The Writings of Mark Twain*, Definitive Edition, V (New York, 1922), 210–211.
6. *A Little Journey in the World* (New York, 1889), p. 37.
7. *A Little Journey*, pp. 242–243.
8. *A Little Journey*, pp. 243–244.
9. *A Little Journey*, p. 227. Mr. Morgan says that Jerry Hollowell "represents the democratic plutocracy that we are coming to."
10. *A Hazard of New Fortunes*, Dolphin Books, p. 387.
11. Howells' comment in 1909, quoted by Clara M. Kirk, "Reality and Actuality in the March Family Narratives of W. D. Howells," PMLA, LXXIV (March, 1959), 148.
12. *Ibid.*, LXXIV, 142.
13. *A Hazard of New Fortunes*, p. 399.
14. *Ibid.*, p. 271.

15. The sentiment is Conrad Dryfoos', but Howells evidently shares it (*A Hazard of New Fortunes*, p. 131).
16. *A Hazard of New Fortunes*, p. 400.
17. *Ibid.*, p. 309.
18. *Ibid.*, p. 400.
19. *Idem.*
20. *Ibid.*, p. 230.
21. For example, *ibid.*, p. 369. Howells speaks of transactions on the Stock Exchange as "the betting" and "the game."
22. *Ibid.*, p. 197.
23. *Ibid.*, p. 387.
24. *Ibid.*, p. 162.
25. *Ibid.*, p. 402.
26. *Ibid.*, p. 198.
27. *Ibid.*, pp. 81–82.
28. *Ibid.*, p. 157.
29. *Ibid.*, p. 286.
30. *Ibid.*, p. 126.

Chapter 2

1. *A Connecticut Yankee in King Arthur's Court* (facsimile of the first edition), ed. Hamlin Hill (San Francisco, 1963), p. 20.
2. SLC to Clara Clemens, Hartford, July 1890, in *The Love Letters of Mark Twain*, ed. Dixon Wecter (New York, 1949), p. 257.
3. The theory of history embodied in *A Connecticut Yankee* is discussed by Roger B. Salomon in *Twain and the Image of History* (New Haven, 1961), Chapter VI, "The Fall of Prometheus."
4. "The Course of Composition of *A Connecticut Yankee:* A Reinterpretation," *American Literature*, XXXIII (May, 1961), 195–214.
5. Notebook #18, October 24, 1884–April 4, 1885, typescript, p. 11, Mark Twain Papers, University of California Library, Berkeley.
6. The burlesque *Hamlet* is in Mark Twain Papers, DV 320.
7. Notebook #18, typescript, p. 17.
8. He described his visit in a dispatch to the San Francisco *Alta*

California dated 25 January 1868: "It must have required more brains to invent all those things than would serve to stock fifty Senates like ours. I took a living interest in that birth-place of six-shooters, because I had seen so many graceful specimens of their performances in the deadfalls of Washoe and California.

"They showed us the new battery gun on wheels—the Gatling gun, or rather, it is a cluster of six to ten savage tubes that carry great conical pellets of lead, with unerring accuracy, a distance of two and a half miles. It feeds itself with cartridges, and you work it with a crank like a hand organ; you can fire it faster than four men can count. When fired rapidly, the reports blend together like the clattering of a watchman's rattle. It can be discharged four hundred times in a minute! I liked it very much, and went on grinding it as long as they could afford cartridges for the amusement—which was not very long" (*The Twainian*, September–October 1948, p. 4).

9. Notebook #20, August 20, 1885–January 20, 1886, typescript, p. 34.

10. *Ibid.*, p. 33.

11. The Yankee is called "Sir Bob Smith" in the report in the New York *Herald* (12 November 1886, p. 10, cols. 1–2), and "Sir Robert Smith" in the *Sun* (reprinted in Hartford *Courant*, 13 November 1886, p. 1, cols. 6–7). The name is "Hank Smith" in undated manuscript notes for the book (Paine 91, Mark Twain Papers).

12. This passage is quoted with a few unimportant variants in the *Sun* report, but for the sake of consistency I follow the first edition of the book (p. 20).

13. Also, with minor variants, in the *Sun* report; first edition, p. 36.

14. From the *Sun* report (Hartford *Courant*, p. 1, col. 7).

15. The *Herald* report, for example, says that the Yankee "was sent by King Arthur to capture a castle, kill the ogre and set at liberty sixty princesses in regular knightly style. Sir Bob comments upon this:—'Well, of all the damn contracts this is the boss. Why, I offered to sublet it to Sir Launcelot at ninety days and no margin. But no, he'd got a better thing' . . . he arms himself with a lasso. He doesn't tackle the ogre, but goes back and tells

a majestic lie about it like the rest of the Knights, and the King thinks it's all right and that he has sent to their homes the released princesses, C. O. D. He easily discounts the simple Knights of the Round Table in lying about his achievements, showing what an educated nineteenth century man can do in the lofty realms of that art, and becomes a favorite of the King and finally the boss of the kingdom" (12 November 1886, p. 10, col. 1). The evolution of the Yankee in folklore is traced by Walter Blair in the Introduction to his anthology, *Native American Humor (1800–1900)* (New York, 1937), esp. pp. 38–62. The "tarnal cuteness" of the Yankee is mentioned on p. 29, and on p. 27n. Mr. Blair notes that "on the Illinois frontier in the forties, a verb, 'yankee,' in general use, meant 'to cheat' or 'to gild.' "

16. Hartford, 16 November 1886, in *Mark Twain to Mrs. Fairbanks,* ed. Dixon Wecter, San Marino, Calif., 1949, pp. 257–258.

17. Quoted in the *Sun* report; first edition, p. 43.

18. *A Connecticut Yankee,* pp. 43–44 (not quoted in the *Sun*).

19. *Ibid.,* p. 77.

20. *Ibid.,* p. 113.

21. *Ibid.,* p. 85.

22. *Ibid.,* pp. 95–96. The Yankee's comparison of himself to Joseph can be glossed by a passage from Mark Twain's burlesque version of the Old Testament account, contained in a dispatch to the *Alta California* published on 12 January 1868: "Then did Joseph show what manner of man he was. He beared the market and bought all the corn that was to be raised in Egypt for seven years to come, and stored it away. And when the first year of the famine was approaching he bought again at six months, buyer's option, and surprised the boys very greatly, for when he called his stocks they could not deliver. In that day many a man sold short and Joseph had them on the hip, and their names were posted and they forfeited their seats in the Board. And during all those years of famine, ships came from far countries that were in distress, and lo, the corn that Joseph bought at forty cents he sold it unto them at seven dollars and a half. Before a time and a half or two times had passed over

their heads, Joseph and Pharaoh owned about two-thirds of Egypt; and it is estimated that if Pharaoh could have dreamed one more dream and got Joseph to interpret it, they would have shortly owned the balance of it" (reprinted in Daniel M. McKeithan, ed., *Traveling With the Innocents Abroad,* Norman, Okla., 1958, p. 223).

23. *A Connecticut Yankee,* pp. 88, 90–91.

24. *Ibid.,* pp. 117–118.

25. *Ibid.,* pp. 420–425.

26. SLC to Theodore W. Crane, Hartford, 5 October 1888, in *Mark Twain's Letters,* ed. Albert B. Paine, 2 vols. (New York, 1917), II, 500–501.

27. *Idem.*

28. Charles S. Holmes, "*A Connecticut Yankee in King Arthur's Court:* Mark Twain's Fable of Uncertainty," *South Atlantic Quarterly,* LXI (Autumn, 1962), 462–472, esp. p. 467.

29. James M. Cox, "*A Connecticut Yankee in King Arthur's Court:* the Machinery of Self-Preservation," *Yale Review,* L (Autumn, 1960), 89–102, reprinted in *Mark Twain: A Collection of Critical Essays,* ed. Henry N. Smith (Englewood Cliffs, N. J., 1963), pp. 117–129. I have used a number of suggestions from this essay and that by Mr. Holmes.

30. SLC to Orion Clemens, Hartford, 5 January 1889, in *Mark Twain's Letters,* II, 508. Mr. Holmes notes the parallel with the Yankee's factories and workshops.

31. *A Connecticut Yankee,* pp. 280–281.

32. *Ibid.,* pp. 532–533.

33. *Ibid.,* p. 538.

34. *Ibid.,* p. 551.

Chapter 3

1. A half-dozen recent studies bearing on the figure of the American Adam are discussed by Frederic I. Carpenter in " 'The American Myth': Paradise (to Be) Regained," *PMLA,* LXXIV (December, 1959), 599–606.

2. Louis J. Budd assembles evidence concerning Mark Twain's

Anglophobia in *Mark Twain: Social Philosopher*, Bloomington, Indiana, 1962, pp. 118–144.

3. Howard M. Jones, "Arnold, Aristocracy, and America," *American Historical Review*, XLIX (April, 1944), 393–409.

4. "Civilisation in the United States," published in *Nineteenth Century*, April, 1888; reprinted in *Representative Essays of Matthew Arnold*, ed. E. K. Brown (New York, 1936), p. 222. Mark Twain's irritation at Arnold's criticism of the United States is documented in John B. Hoben, "Mark Twain's *A Connecticut Yankee*: A Genetic Study," *American Literature*, XVIII (November, 1946), 197–218.

5. Howard G. Baetzhold, "Mark Twain: England's Advocate," *American Literature*, XVIII (November, 1956), 328–346.

6. [Hartford, 1889], in *Mark Twain's Letters*, II, 525–528.

7. 18 January 1890, clipping in "Mark Twain Papers."

8. 13 January 1890, clipping in "Mark Twain Papers."

9. *A Connecticut Yankee*, p. 525.

10. *Ibid.*, p. 573. Uncle Sam was, of course, historically derived from the Yankee of folklore.

11. *Ibid.*, pp. 372–373.

12. SLC to Messrs. Chatto & Windus, in *Mark Twain's Letters*, II, 524.

13. "Mark Twain's New Book. A Satirical Attack on English Institutions" (editorial introduction to a condensed version of *A Yankee at the Court of King Arthur* [title of the English edition]), *Review of Reviews* (London), I (February, 1890), 144. Stead said that the book's "cumbrous and strenuous moralizing . . . makes it at times more like one of Jonathan Edwards' sermons than a mere buoyant and farcical bubbling up of American humour."

14. *Plumas National*, 5 July 1890, p. 2.

15. Beard to SLC, New York, 12 November 1889, in Mark Twain Papers.

16. Boston *Herald*, 15 December 1889, p. 17, col. 1.

17. In "The Editor's Study," *Harper's*, LXXX (January, 1890), 319–321.

18. New York, 7 July 1889, in Mark Twain Papers.

19. *A Connecticut Yankee*, p. 473.

20. New York *Standard*, Vol. VII, No. 1, 1 January 1890, p. 10.

21. *A Connecticut Yankee*, p. 101.

22. *Ibid.*, pp. 41, 279, 297.

23. For example, in an interview published in the New York *Times*, 10 December 1889, p. 5.

24. Salomon, *Twain and the Image of History*, ch. I ("History and the American Writer"), ch. II ("Twain and the Whig Hypothesis").

25. Budd, *Mark Twain: Social Philosopher*, pp. 89–90.

26. Henry N. Smith, *Mark Twain: The Development of a Writer*, Cambridge, Mass., 1962, pp. 174–175.

27. *A Connecticut Yankee*, p. 387.

28. Henry N. Smith, *Mark Twain: The Development of a Writer*, pp. 156–157.

29. DV 21, in Mark Twain Papers. The word "magic" has been canceled.

30. *A Connecticut Yankee*, p. 541.

31. "Have We Appropriated France's Civilization?" DV 317, in Mark Twain Papers. Mr. Salomon comments on the definition of civilization implied here (*Twain and the Image of History*, pp. 31–32).

32. *A Connecticut Yankee*, p. 89.

33. In the Preface to the second edition of *Lyrical Ballads* (1800).

34. *A Connecticut Yankee*, p. 120.

35. *Ibid.*, p. 159.

36. *Mark Twain: Social Philosopher*, pp. 113, 137–144. Mr. Budd points out that Mark Twain's position closely resembled that of Andrew Carnegie and of many English Liberals (pp. 120–122, 132–136).

37. *A Connecticut Yankee*, pp. 334–336, 281–282.

38. *Ibid.*, p. 532.

39. *Ibid.*, p. 465.

40. New York *Times*, 10 December 1889, p. 5.

41. Untitled MS, DV 127, in Mark Twain Papers. Copyright © 1964, Mark Twain Company.

42. The most recent summary account of Adams' "failure" is

Chapter IX of George Hochfield, *Henry Adams: An Introduction and Interpretation*, New York, 1962, pp. 115–139. Rele-
vant also in this connection is Tony Tanner's "The Lost America—The Despair of Henry Adams and Mark Twain," *Modern
Age*, V (Summer, 1961), 299–310, reprinted in *Mark Twain: A
Collection of Critical Essays*, ed. Henry N. Smith, pp. 159–174.

43. "The New Dynasty," in Paul J. Carter, Jr., "Mark Twain and
the American Labor Movement," *New England Quarterly*,
XXX (September, 1957), 382–388.

44. "My works showed what a despot could do with the resources
of a kingdom at his command" (*A Connecticut Yankee*, pp.
119–120).

45. Henry N. Smith, *Virgin Land: The American West as Symbol
and Myth*, Cambridge, Mass., 1950, pp. 257–260.

46. Mark Twain's impatience of restraint was deeper than the contrast of civilizations. In the original dream it was the armor, the
symbol not of modern technology but of medieval civilization
(especially tyranny?), that was so uncomfortable for the
dreamer.

47. Bernard Bowron, Leo Marx, and Arnold Rose, "Literature and
Covert Culture," *American Quarterly*, IX (Winter, 1957),
382–383.

48. *A Connecticut Yankee*, p. 574.

49. *Eros and Civilization: A Philosophical Inquiry into Freud*,
Boston, 1955.

50. *A Connecticut Yankee*, p. 538.

51. *Ibid.*, p. 217.

52. *Ibid.*, p. 574.

passing silohuttes of
houses (in rows) -
streetlights shining
in between the stars
between clouds fall
to ground.

---

scene in story - writing in
deserted train carriage -
late - dark at night -
isolated, anything
could happen..

.. though alone - you feel
vulnerable too - if you
let your imagination wander

another train - passing by outside
- burst of light - makes
taste it him jump raises heart -
in your throat. adrenalin - pulse - just
a little